# THE SAFETY OF GOD'S SECRET PLACE

Copyright © 2024 by Jeremy D. Kiser

Published by Dream Releaser Publishing

All rights reserved. No portion of this book may be reproduced, stored in a retrieval system, or transmitted in any form or by any means—electronic, mechanical, photocopy, recording, scanning, or other—except for brief quotations in critical reviews or articles, without prior written permission of the author.

Unless otherwise specified, all Scripture quotations are taken from the New King James Version®. Copyright © 1982 by Thomas Nelson. Used by permission. All rights reserved. | Scripture quotations marked ESV are from The ESV® Bible (The Holy Bible, English Standard Version®), copyright © 2001 by Crossway, a publishing ministry of Good News Publishers. Used by permission. All rights reserved. | Scripture quotations marked KJV are taken from the King James Version of the Bible. Public domain. | Scripture quotations marked NASB are taken from the (NASB®) New American Standard Bible®, Copyright © 1960, 1971, 1977, 1995, 2020 by The Lockman Foundation. Used by permission. All rights reserved. www.lockman.org | Scripture quotations marked NASB 1995 are taken from the (NASB®) New American Standard Bible 1995®, Copyright © 1960, 1971, 1977, 1995, by The Lockman Foundation. Used by permission. All rights reserved. www.lockman.org | Scripture quotations marked NIRV are taken from the New International Reader's Version (NIRV), copyright © 1995, 1996, 1998, 2014 by Biblica, Inc. ®. Used by permission. All rights reserved worldwide. | Scripture quotations marked NIV are taken from the Holy Bible, New International Version®, NIV®. Copyright © 1973, 1978, 1984, 2011 by Biblica, Inc.™ Used by permission of Zondervan. All rights reserved worldwide. www.zondervan.com. The "NIV" and "New International Version" are trademarks registered in the United States Patent and Trademark Office by Biblica, Inc.™ | Scripture quotations marked NLT are taken from the Holy Bible, New Living Translation, copyright © 1996, 2004, 2015 by Tyndale House Foundation. Used by permission of Tyndale House Publishers, Inc., Carol Stream, Illinois 60188. All rights reserved. | Copyright © 2015 by The Lockman Foundation, La Habra, CA 90631. All rights reserved. The "Amplified" trademark (AMP) is registered in the United States Patent and Trademark Office by The Lockman Foundation. Use of this trademark requires the permission of The Lockman Foundation.

For foreign and subsidiary rights, contact the author.

Cover design by Sara Young
Cover photo by Carolina Rose Photography

ISBN: 978-1-962401-77-7      1 2 3 4 5 6 7 8 9 10

Printed in the United States of America

JEREMY D. KISER

# LIVING IN THE SAFETY OF GOD'S SECRET PLACE

## STAYING DEVILPROOF: THE SAFEST PLACE FOR YOUR SOUL

*Dedicated to my dear mother who raised us in the admonition of the Lord, who's heart and spirit continue to inspire and live inside of me.*

*Dedicated to my dear wife Isabel and to my sister Angel (a.k.a "Red") and to my brother Daniel.*

*Dedicated to that dear person—you are so loved and treasured by God.*

# CONTENTS

## PART 1. REALITIES OF THE SPIRIT REALM: SPIRITUAL FACTORS THAT IMPACT YOUR SOUL..........9

- CHAPTER 1. Do You Need Insurance or Assurance?..... 11
- CHAPTER 2. Evidence of God's Existence............. 15
- CHAPTER 3. The Nature and Attributes of God........ 25
- CHAPTER 4. The Trinity........................ 33
- CHAPTER 5. Jesus Christ........................ 37
- CHAPTER 6. The Holy Spirit..................... 45
- CHAPTER 7. Angels and Demons.................. 47

## PART 2. UNDERSTANDING THE CONDITION OF YOUR SOUL..........59

- CHAPTER 8. The Ultimate Bad News, Good News Scenario......................... 61

## PART 3. KNOWING GOD PERSONALLY: MAKING YOUR SOUL SECURE IN GOD.......73

- CHAPTER 9. Your Secret Admirer!.................. 75
- CHAPTER 10. Knowing God Through Faith........... 77
- CHAPTER 11. Knowing God Through Jesus Christ...... 79
- CHAPTER 12. Knowing God by His Word............. 83
- CHAPTER 13. Knowing God Through Suffering........ 95
- CHAPTER 14. Knowing God by His Holy Spirit........ 97
- CHAPTER 15. Knowing God by His Voice............ 101

## PART 4. ABIDING IN THE SAFETY OF GOD'S SECRET PLACE ................................ 121

- **CHAPTER 16.** Keeping Your Soul Secure in God ....... 123
- **CHAPTER 17.** Practical Application #1: A Strong Prayer Life ....................... 129
- **CHAPTER 18.** Practical Application #2: Fasting ....... 145
- **CHAPTER 19.** Practical Application #3: Genuine and True Worship................... 149
- **CHAPTER 20.** Practical Application #4: Genuine Praise. 155
- **CHAPTER 21.** Practical Application #5: Abiding in Christ........................ 159
- **CHAPTER 22.** Practical Application #6: Confession and Repentance of Sin ............... 161
- **CHAPTER 23.** Practical Application #7: Walking with and Abiding in God's Love ............ 167
- **CHAPTER 24.** Practical Application #8: Holiness (Consecration)..................... 173
- **CHAPTER 25.** Practical Application #9: Brokenness.... 175
- **CHAPTER 26.** Practical Application #10: Putting on the Full Armor of God ............ 183

*Practical Applications Summary* ......................... 203

# PART 1

# REALITIES OF THE SPIRIT REALM: SPIRITUAL FACTORS THAT IMPACT YOUR SOUL

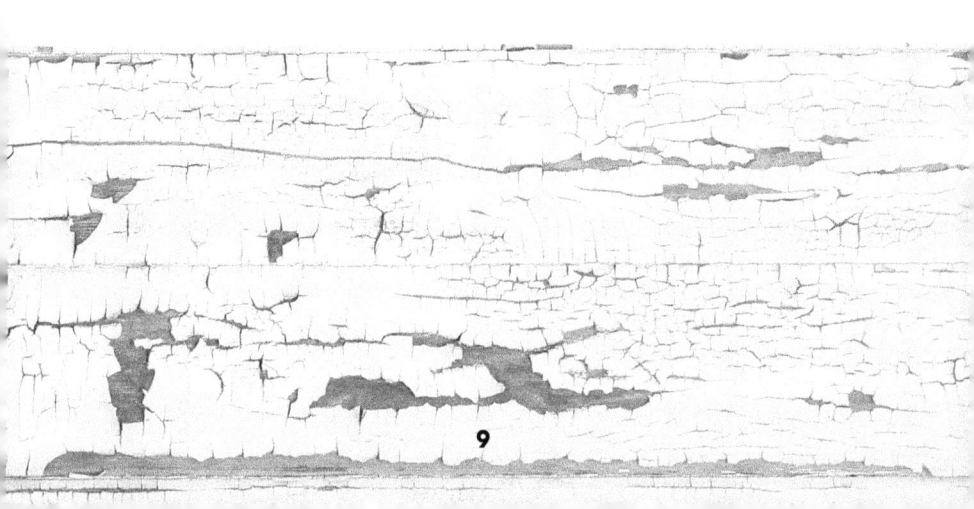

# CHAPTER 1

# DO YOU NEED INSURANCE OR ASSURANCE?

Are you secure enough? Do you need insurance or assurance for security and protection? From the highest levels of government to our own personal lives, everybody wants security and protection—and rightly so! My late mother had four shotguns in the closet, God forbid a thief or intruder were to break into our house. In our country we have the National Security Council (NSC) which oversees policy and advises the government on issues of national security; even the National Security Advisor (NSA) serves as a senior aide to the president on matters of National Security. Working as an electrical engineer by trade at several power plants, I learned that cyber security, designed to prevent unauthorized access to the plant's network data and systems, is one of the many security measures in place. Beyond that, other personnel (i.e., security guards with guns) serve as protection for the plant. At the airport, the Transportation Security Administration (TSA) is in charge of preventing prohibited items (or people) from entering the sterile area of the airport and other threats to transportation. I'm a die-hard Clemson Tiger football fan and alumni; in all of the games I have attended (and will attend), I cannot enter (or leave) a game without going through security guards (and measures).

What am I saying? It's true that having security is very important and a high priority! All of us have a legitimate need and desire for personal protection and security, and for our families and possessions like our property and valued assets that are very important to us. Part of gaining protection and security for anything is to understand the risk and threat; for instance, many of us have a security system for our home to help prevent the threat of a break-in; many of us have iPhone protectors to eliminate the risk and threat of breaking our phones; many of us use an umbrella to eliminate the risk and threat of getting wet if it rains; many of us use sunscreen at the beach to eliminate the risk and threat of sunburn. We understand and fear the risk and threat of what can happen if and when we don't have protection and security.

We even get insurance policies for our life, health, finances, homes, property/possessions, and family among other things that are important to us. But what is even more valuable and in greatest need of security and protection?

What about your soul?

If someone were to ask you right now: "How much security and protection do you have for your soul?" what would you say? Your soul is the most valuable and important thing to God because His great love for you cannot be measured or put into words. What I can say is this: you were worth Him sending His one and only Son to die for you (see John 3:16) so your soul could escape hell fire (see Revelation 21:8) and have eternal life with Him! (see Romans 6:23) Yes, God's love for your soul is unquestionable! But the real question is, how valuable and important to *you* is your soul? The most tragic loss would be to have everything the world has to offer—all the luxury, goods, comforts, security, and protection you could ever have in this life—and lose your very soul in hellfire for eternity! Also, unlike many of the temporal and tangible things that we might insure, **you cannot purchase INSURANCE for your soul!** However, fortunately, by God's grace, you can acquire ASSURANCE for it!

To have insurance for the present life but no assurance for this life or the afterlife is the greatest risk, threat, and danger of all! Insurance may provide you with compensation in the event of damages and/or losses, but it is God's assurance that will preserve your soul, both in this life and in the afterlife! Psalm 91:1 says: "He who dwells in the secret place of the Most High shall abide under the shadow of the Almighty." This psalm is an awesome passage of Scripture that promises God's security and protection for those who live in His secret place and names the benefits of God's security and protection. This book is about understanding the risks and threats against your soul, understanding the condition of your soul, making your soul secure in God, and keeping it secure in God, not only for the afterlife but in this present life. **With all the trials and tribulations of life, your very soul can be made secure in God! You can be devil-proof!**

Table 1 illustrates the differences between insurance and assurance.

| INSURANCE | ASSURANCE |
|---|---|
| A policy purchased with money based on credentials. | A covenant purchased with the blood of Christ based on His credentials. |
| Covers temporary things in this life. | Covers and protects your soul unto eternity. |
| Can be cancelled (i.e., with lapses of payment). | Assurance can never be cancelled or annulled because the blood of Christ paid for it in full once and for all (Hebrews 7:27). |
| Insurance claims for benefits can be rejected, denied, and/or paid out slowly in the event of damages and/or losses. | All of God's promises, blessings, benefits, and privileges are available and irrevocable to you from the event of Christ's death, burial, and resurrection and the moment you place your faith in Him as Savior and Lord. |

TABLE 1: **INSURANCE VS. ASSURANCE**

# CHAPTER 2

# EVIDENCE OF GOD'S EXISTENCE

The French poet Charles Baudelaire once wrote: "The greatest trick the devil ever played was convincing the world he did not exist." I would echo this statement by saying the greatest prank a person can ever play on themselves is to intelligently and rationally convince themselves that God does not exist.

All of us are very aware and familiar with the physical world. Every day we can see, hear, taste, touch, and smell the physical world around us. Yet beyond this physical world of ours is also the reality of a spiritual world (or spirit realm) that we cannot see with our natural sight. Even though we cannot see the spiritual world, it is just as real as the physical world that we do see. God made you as a three-part being: body, soul, and spirit (see 1 Thessalonians 5:23). Our body is the physical, material part of us that interacts with the physical world, whereas the soul and spirit are the immaterial parts of us. Specifically, our souls are the essence of our being, consisting of our mind, will, and emotions, and our spirit is the other immaterial part of us that commune with God.

To make your soul secure and safe, you must understand the immaterial risks and threats from the spirit realm that can come against it as well as the right type of protection and security needed to guard it. This involves recognizing how the spiritual world impacts and affects the physical world and even your personal life (your very soul).

The spiritual world includes God, angels, and demons. The Bible says that God is a Spirit (see John 4:24), which means that He is an immaterial being and cannot be seen (with natural sight). The Bible also says that no man has seen God (see John 1:18; 1 John 4:20). Angels and demons are also spirits (see Hebrews 1:14; Matthew 8:16). We cannot fully comprehend, describe, or define who God is. However, we can say that God is the sovereign being and Creator of all creation (see Colossians 1:16). God as sovereign means that He has all power, all knowledge, and all authority to do anything He wishes or chooses concerning His creation. A question that often arises is, how do we know that God exists? I would challenge this question with my own question: how can we not know that God exists? Generally, we can consider three main things that affirm the existence of God:

1) General revelation
2) Special revelation
3) Human conscience

## GENERAL REVELATION

"General revelation" is what God has revealed about Himself through creation. Psalms 19:1-4 (NASB 1995) says:

*The heavens are telling of the glory of God; And their expanse is declaring the work of His hands. Day to day pours forth speech, and night to night reveals knowledge. There is no speech, nor are there words; Their voice is not heard.*

Romans 1:18-20 (NASB 1995) also states:

*"For since the creation of the world His invisible attributes, His eternal power and divine nature, have been clearly seen, being understood through what has been made, so that they are without excuse."*

## Anthropological: *Intelligent Life Comes from an Intelligent God*

"Anthropos" is a Greek word that means "man." God made His most prized and precious creation when He said: "Let us make man in our image, after our likeness" (Genesis 1:26, ESV). The one thing that makes us unique and distinct from any other creature that God created—from the animals to the angels—is the fact that we were made and created in the image of God (Imago Dei). This means we are creatures with a spirit who can commune and fellowship with God; we have intelligence and the ability to think, reason, rationalize, and show emotion. The intelligence of man is one of the greatest pieces of evidence for the existence of an intelligent, supreme God and Creator; every human being bears the mark of God's existence and creatorship.

## Biological: *Life Comes from a Life-Giving Source, Who is God*

The word "bios" in the Greek language means "life." It is a fact of science that life can only come from pre-existing life; life cannot come from matter. Therefore, all life must be traced back to God, who is the ultimate Source, Giver, and Creator.

## Cosmological: *The Universe and Man Exist According to the Cause and Purpose of God*

"Cosmos" is a Greek word that means "world." Cosmological evidence for God's existence is based on the law of "cause and effect." We understand that there is a cause behind everything that exists. For example, if you walk into a room and see an iPhone sitting on a table, you'll understand that someone had to put it there; someone is responsible for its placement. Furthermore, you understand that someone caused the iPhone to exist (i.e., iPhone engineer/designer). Based on that same law of cause and effect, we should also recognize that someone (a sovereign being and Creator) caused the existence of the world and the universe. It's not by coincidence or by chance that the world and universe exist, just like your iPhone doesn't exist by coincidence or chance. (It didn't appear out of thin air.)

## Teleological: *Design Reflects the Brilliance and Existence of the Creative God*

Teleological evidence for God's existence considers the genius design and purpose of the created world and universe. Could you have a house without a builder or architect? Could you possess an iPhone, iPad, TV, computer, or car, without a designer/inventor? Personally, as an engineer, I have an appreciation for good designs. There are times when I'll look at an invention or the work of another engineer and say: "Wow . . . that is a good design and really needed! Whoever came up with that was brilliant!" I would imagine you have had the same experience and have made similar statements. A good design affirms the brilliance and existence of the person who designed it. Therefore, when we consider how the world was designed with such precision to allow for the existence and sustaining power of human life, we should recognize that there is a supreme, intelligent designer (God) behind the creation of the world and the universe. Let's consider some of the parameters necessary for human life to exist sustain.

In the 1960s, an astronomer by the name of Carl Sagan explained that one requirement for life to exist on a planet is that it must be at a certain distance from a star, like the sun. Since that time, scientists have discovered more and more required conditions for human life to exist on a planet. Dr Hugh Ross, an astrophysicist, noted 200 conditions that must all be met for a planet to sustain human life. The first is water. The earth is positioned precisely where it needs to be in space relative to the sun for water to exist. If the earth was just as little as 2 percent closer or further from the sun, there wouldn't be any water. The earth makes a complete 360-degree rotation on its axis every twenty-four hours; if the earth rotated any slower, we would all freeze to death. If it rotated any faster, we would all die from overheating. Have you ever wondered why certain planets are of certain sizes and positioned where they are in outer space? For instance, if Jupiter wasn't the size that it is and positioned where it is in space, meteors might strike the earth, resulting in worldwide calamity and death. If Jupiter was any bigger, its gravitational force on the earth would suck the earth out of orbit and kill us. So, either we believe these precise conditions needed for human life exist by coincidence or chance, or we believe a transcendent supreme intelligent being designer/engineer is behind it all!

## SPECIAL REVELATION

Special revelation is how God reveals Himself through supernatural or miraculous means. Examples of special revelation are theophanies, Jesus Christ, and the Bible (God's Word).

### Theophanies

A theophany is a physical appearance or manifestation of God. There are many examples of theophanies in the Old Testament where God physically appeared in many forms: as a pillar of cloud by day and a pillar of fire by night to guide the children of Israel in the wilderness (see Exodus 13:21-22); as an angel when He visited Abraham (see Genesis 18:1-33); and as a burning bush to Moses (see Exodus 3:2). God's walk through the Garden of Eden in the cool of the day before Adam and Eve sinned may be a theophany (see Genesis 3:8). Of course, in the New Testament, God's ultimate physical appearance and manifestation came in the person of Jesus Christ (see John 1:1-2, 14; Colossians 1:15).

### Jesus Christ

Jesus Christ is the full expression and complete revelation of the invisible God as Colossians 1:15 says: "He [Jesus Christ] is the image of the invisible God, the firstborn over all creation." Furthermore, Jesus was (is) God incarnate in flesh (see Isaiah 7:14; John 1:1, 14; 14:1-11; Colossians 2:9; Hebrews 1:1-3). Jesus Christ is also equated to being the Word of God (The Bible) as the Gospel of John 1:1, 14 (NASB 1995) says: "In the beginning was the Word, and the Word was with God, and the Word was God.... And the Word became flesh, and dwelt among us, and we saw His glory, glory as of the only begotten from the Father, full of grace and truth." A prophecy about Jesus Christ in Isaiah 7:14 (NLT) also states: "The virgin will conceive a child. She will give birth to a son and will call him Immanuel (which means 'God is with us')." The significance of what "Immanuel" really means is found in understanding what the celebration of Christmas is all about—the most special time in human history. It was on this day that God actually became human and dwelled among us in the person of Jesus Christ. It was at this time that Jesus, as God in the flesh, walked the earth to identify and relate to our human struggles and sympathize with us. It was then that Jesus began His early journey into manhood. He grew tired, weary, sleepy, and hungry. He cried, expressed emotions, felt our pain, and was (is) compassionate to feed us, heal us, deliver us, and set us free. He took the full wrath of our punishment for our sins upon Himself, so that we may have eternal life with God. For more, reference Chapter 5: Jesus Christ

## The Bible

The Bible is special revelation of God—His nature, His character, His redemptive history, and His plans and will for mankind. The Bible is unique and unlike any other book or writing because it is "God-breathed" (2 Timothy 2:16-17); in other words, it is the only "divinely inspired" book or writing.

- **Inspiration:** In the Bible, you will find the recorded history of God using ordinary and flawed human beings to work His will. Even though people in the Bible were just like us (flawed, imperfect, etc.), God used them and divinely inspired the authors of the Bible to write what is known to be the Scriptures, as the Apostle Paul writes in his letter to Timothy: "All Scripture [in the Bible] is given by inspiration of God, and is profitable for sound teaching, for reproof, for correction, for instruction in righteousness" 2 Timothy 3:16-17 (author paraphrase). Therefore, the inspiration of the Bible involved God's divine superintendence of human authors through the inspiration of the Holy Spirit, working with their personalities, skill sets, and experiences. The holy Scriptures of the Bible were composed, written, and recorded without error as God's revelation to man. In other words, the Bible is divinely produced by God Himself through imperfect and sinful men. Yet, their writings were infallible because they were written by the inspiration of the Holy Spirit to reveal the God of the Bible.

- **The Inerrancy of the Bible:** Because the Bible is "God-breathed" (inspired by God), we know that it is also inerrant; it does not affirm anything contrary to fact. The Bible is truthful in all its teaching and revelation; it always tells the truth concerning everything, so it is without error or contradiction.
- **The Authority of the Bible:** Because the Bible is divinely inspired by God and without error, it is also authentic as the ultimate source of all authority and truth both to and for mankind.

## HUMAN CONSCIENCE

An inner witness or an intuitive knowing of God's existence, as well as an inner sense of right and wrong, has been placed inside of every human being. This inner witness is the human conscience described in Romans 1:18-20 (NASB 1995):

> For the wrath of God is revealed from heaven against all ungodliness and unrighteousness of men who suppress the truth in unrighteousness, because that which is known about God is evident within them; for God made it evident to them. For since the creation of the world His invisible attributes, His eternal power and divine nature, have been clearly seen, being understood through what has been made, so that they are without excuse.

This is why, in reality, there are no atheists. Someone once said: "An atheist cannot find God for the same reason that a thief can't find a policeman," because they're not looking to find God any more than a thief would be looking to find the police. Just because someone isn't looking to find God does not mean He doesn't exist. Atheism only ignores or rejects the evidence of God's existence through attempts to suppress their inner, intuitive knowing and truth. David said in Psalm 14:1 (KJV) that "The fool hath said in his heart, *There is* no God."

## THE EXISTENCE OF GOD

General revelation, special revelation, and human conscience all affirm the existence of God. Yet even though God's existence is affirmed through general revelation (i.e., creation) and the human conscience, man can't come to a personal knowing and true knowledge of God without special revelation (i.e., through the Bible and Jesus Christ). Those special revelations—the Bible and Jesus Christ—are what bring us to a true, personal knowledge and knowing of God.

Belief in the existence of God is essential and foundational to a personal knowing and understanding of God and to life itself. Hebrews 11:6 says, "He who comes to God must believe that He is [that He exists], and *that* He is a rewarder of those who diligently seek Him." **In other words, belief in the existence of God is a prerequisite to having faith in God and knowing God personally.**

# CHAPTER 3

# THE NATURE AND ATTRIBUTES OF GOD

It is God who takes the initiative to reveal Himself to man (see Matthew 11:27). It is also God who, even before the creation of the world, predetermined to choose man for Himself to be holy and without blame before Him in love (see Ephesians 1:3-6) and have a relationship with Him (see Jeremiah 1:6). Mankind is incapable of seeking after God and loving Him without the conviction and power of the Holy Spirit (see Psalm 14:1-3; Psalm 53:1-3; John 16:8-15; Romans 3:10-12, 5:5; Galatians 5:22-23). **As I mentioned in the last chapter, while general revelation and the human conscience testify of the existence of God, it is impossible for** man to come to a true understanding and personal knowing of God without the special revelation of

God as revealed in the Scriptures. The following gives a few basic descriptions of God's nature from the Scriptures:

**God Is a Spirit**

The Bible says that God is a Spirit (see John 4:24); He is immaterial, incorporeal, and invisible (see John 1:18; 1 Timothy 1:17; Colossians 1:15), not like a physical person with flesh and bones who we can see and touch, but a Spirit being. Nevertheless, God is spoken of as being a person and not some impersonal force (see 1 John 3:1). Also, even though God is Spirit, He is capable of and has manifested in physical form (i.e., mainly by theophanies and in Jesus Christ).

**God Is Light**

The Bible says that God is light (see 1 John 1:5), and He dwells in unapproachable light that no man has seen nor can see (see 1 Timothy 6:15-16), which is absolutely pure, holy, and undefiled. God's light is not like the light that we know (see Revelation 21:23). Metaphorically, those who find God's light are enlightened by His Word and His truth (see Psalm 119:105; Romans 8:12; Ephesians 5:8; 1 Thessalonians 5:4-5).

**God Is Love**

Love is the essence of who God is, the very core of God's nature (see 1 John 4:17). God not only demonstrates His love; He *is* love (see 1 John 4:7-8). The love of God is shown in His grace, mercy, kindness, goodness, and benevolence towards all His creation, and especially towards mankind, His most prized and cherished creation (see John 3:16)

## ATTRIBUTES OF GOD

Attributes are defined as characteristics or traits that belong to a person and make them who they are. Therefore, attributes of God are those characteristics or traits that belong to God and make God who and what He is. Two categories are used to describe the attributes of God: moral (communicable) attributes and essential (incommunicable attributes).

**Moral (Communicable) Attributes**

The moral or communicable attributes of God are the characteristics or traits that God shares in relation to mankind; in other words, these are traits of God that mankind can express and reciprocate back to God (though to a lesser degree) and to each other as creatures made in His image.

1) **Holiness:** "Holy" means to be separate, distinct, and set apart. God is infinitely holy (separate, distinct, set apart) from all creation—He is perfect, sinless, sovereign, all-wise, all-knowing, all-powerful, omnipresent, etc. Nobody compares to God; nobody comes close. God has no equal, and as such, He is holy. God also desires for man to be holy as He is holy (see 1 Peter 1:16). Though we can never be holy to the extent that God is, we can live a life of holiness that brings glory and honor to God.

2) **Righteousness:** God's righteousness is His just and right character. God in His righteousness (justice) cannot bear or overlook sin. According to God's righteousness, sin must be judged and punished. Therefore, in the Old Testament, when sin was committed, something had to die or be killed in place of the sinner (typically an animal sacrifice; see

Genesis 3:21; Leviticus 4:1-34) lest the sinner himself die. This is also why the Bible says the wages of sin is death (see Romans 6:23) and without the shedding of blood there can be no remission (forgiveness) of sins (see Hebrews 9:22). In the New Testament, Jesus Christ became the ultimate sacrifice by dying in our place on the cross for our sins to satisfy the righteousness of God against sin (see Romans 8:3-4; 2 Corinthians 5:21; Hebrews 10:10; 1 John 2:2). God's righteousness is reflected in His acts towards man and all of creation. Man's rewards (see Romans 2:7; Hebrews 11:26; Deuteronomy 7:9-13; Psalms 58:11; Matthew 25:21) and punishments (Genesis 2:17; Romans 1:32; 2:8-9) are a result of God's righteousness. Man can also exercise and demonstrate righteousness (justice and being right) in their actions and lifestyle (see Proverbs 2:20; 8:20), albeit to a lesser degree than God.

3) **Love:** Love is God's very nature. God not only has love; God is love (see 1 John 2:7). In our culture, there can be many different meanings to the word love (i.e., "I love my pet," "I love pizza," "I love my car," "I love the Dallas Cowboys," "I love my girlfriend"). Even the Greeks had different words they used to describe love:

- Eros—The romantic and physical attraction type of love.
- Phileo—The brotherly/friendship type of love.
- Agape—The divine, supernatural, unconditional, self-sacrificial type of love.

God's love of us is the "agape" type of love. God ultimately gave His One and Only Son Jesus to die on the cross for our sins to demonstrate this type of love (see John 3:16).

Because we are made in God's image, we can demonstrate and exemplify love towards God, and one another (see Matthew 22:37-39; John 13:34), but we can only demonstrate God's type of love when He gives it to us by His Holy Spirit (see Romans 5:5; Galatians 5:22-23).

Also, we cannot demonstrate agape without giving something of ourselves, as the Bible says: "For God so loved the world that he gave" (John 3:16). The agape type of love is divine and always connected to giving; it is an action, not merely an emotion or word.

4) **Goodness:** God not only does good (shows goodness), but He is good, as Psalms 119:68 (NIV) says: "You are good and what you do is good." God's goodness is evident through creation (see Genesis 1:31). God's goodness is demonstrated in His benevolence (generosity, kindness, grace, mercy, favor) towards us (see Psalms 31:9; 68:10; Matthew 6:26-34, 7:11; Romans 8:32; James 1:17). God as good means there is no evil in Him nor does He ever have evil (bad) motives and intentions (see Deuteronomy 32:4; James 1:13). God always acts in a way that is right and consistent with His nature and character (see Numbers 23:19; Deuteronomy 32:4; Malachi 3:6). Man can also demonstrate goodness towards one another.

5) **Grace:** God's grace is His unlimited kindness and mercy freely given to people who are undeserving or unworthy (see Ephesians 1:2, 6, 7; 2:5-8; 3:2; 2 Timothy 1:2; Titus 1:4; 2 Thessalonians 3:17-18). God's grace also includes His patience, longsuffering, and forbearance towards sinful men (see 2 Peter 3:9; 1 Peter 3:20; Romans 2:4; Exodus 34:6;

Romans 9:22). Man can also show and demonstrate grace (Ephesians 4:29).

6) **Mercy:** Mercy describes how God shows pity for the sinner in his condition (see Ephesians 2:4; James 5:11; Psalm 102:13; Romans 11:30-31; Isaiah 55:7; Luke 1:50, 72; Exodus 20:6; Titus 1:4; 1 Timothy 1:2; 2 Timothy 1:2; Psalm 85:10; Luke 6:36; Matthew 5:45; 2 Peter 3:9). Man can also show and demonstrate mercy (Matthew 5:7).

7) **Compassion:** God's compassion describes His mercy and sympathy for man's needs and sufferings with the motivation to help. Jesus' compassion for others always motivated Him to help them (see Matthew 9:36; 14:14; 18:27; 15:32; Luke 15:20; Psalm 78:28; 86:15; 145:8; 130:7; 103:8-18). Man can also show and demonstrate compassion (see Colossians 3:12).

8) **Kindness:** Kindness speaks of God's benevolence (see Ephesians 2:7; Colossians 3:12; Titus 3:4; Psalm 31:21; Isaiah 54:8, 10; Joel 2:13). Man can also show and demonstrate kindness (see Deuteronomy 15:7-15; Luke 10:33-35).

9) **Faithfulness:** God's faithfulness describes how He is perfectly trustworthy, reliable, and true to His word (see Deuteronomy 7:9, 32:4; Isaiah 25:1, 49:7; Jeremiah 1:12). God cannot lie (see Number 23:19) and His word is always trustworthy, reliable, and true (see Isaiah 55:11). While we cannot express perfect faithfulness as He does, we can show and demonstrate faithfulness (see Proverbs 28:20; 1 Corinthians 4:2).

10) **Creativity:** God is the ultimate Creator as the Bible says He created the heavens and the earth and everything in them (see Genesis 1:31; John 1:3; Colossians 1:16-17). As man,

we can appreciate the glory and beauty of God's creation and creativity (see Psalms 8:1-9, 19:1, 104:1-35; Job 40:1-24; 41:1-34). Being made in God's image and likeness (see Genesis 1:26), we can also be creative. Imagine all of the creations, inventions, innovative engineering accomplishments, and contributions humans have made over the course of history: pyramids, skyscrapers, roads, bridges, vehicles to drive, airplanes to fly in the air, spaceships to go into outer space, electricity, the computer, the iPhone, the iPad, and many other rapid technological advancements.

## Essential (Incommunicable) Attributes

Essential attributes are those attributes or traits that exclusively belong to God that make God who and what He is, apart from every creature. In other words, these are attributes that God does not share with His creatures. Essential attributes of God can never be attributes of man, because that would make man God.

1) **Eternal:** God is eternal in that His existence has no beginning or end; God has always existed from eternity past and will always exist to eternity future as Psalms 90:2 (KJV) says: "From everlasting to everlasting thou art God." Therefore, there has never been a moment or time when God was not (see Isaiah 43:10).

2) **Self-Existence:** God's existence proves that He is the Creator of His own existence and does not owe His existence to anyone else. God is also self-sufficient, which means He is perfectly independent and does not depend on anyone else for sustainability. God describes His self-existence and self-sufficiency as "I AM" (see Exodus 3:14).

3) **Immutability:** God's immutability speaks to His unchanging nature (see Malachi 3:6). God never changes in His nature, character, or being. Hebrews 13:8 says: "Jesus Christ [God] is the same yesterday, today, and forever."
4) **Omnipotent:** God's omnipotence means that He is all-powerful (see Revelation 19:6). Furthermore, God's sovereignty is a testament to His absolute power, control, wisdom, knowledge, and authority over all things. He chooses to do anything He wants to do and permits what He wants to permit (see Genesis 1:1-31; Psalms 33:6; Job 42:2). In other words, nothing can happen that's beyond God's control and beyond what He allows to happen.
5) **Omniscient:** God's omniscience means that He is all-knowing. God has all knowledge of all things past, present, and future. God's knowledge and understanding are infinite and impossible for the human mind to grasp (see Psalms 147:5, Isaiah 40:28). For instance, God knows the precise number of hairs on your head (see Matthew 10:29-30). God knows everything there is to know about Himself and all of His creation.
6) **Omnipresent:** God's omnipresence means that He is present everywhere at the same time (see Psalms 139:7-12; Proverbs 15:3). God is not confined to or limited by space or time.
7) **Perfect:** God's perfection means that He is without any flaws and does not and cannot make mistakes. God is perfect in His nature, in His character, in His word, and in all that He does (see Deuteronomy 32:4; Numbers 23:9; Psalms 18:30; Isaiah 55:11).

# CHAPTER 4

# THE TRINITY

You won't find the word "Trinity" in the Bible, but clearly, the concept and theology of the Trinity is in the Bible. The actual word comes from the Latin term "trinitos" which means "three" or a "triad." Tertullian, a third-century Latin theologian, is historically known as the first person to coin the Latin term to describe how One God exists in three persons: God the Father, God the Son, and God the Holy Spirit. Even though the concept of the Trinity is hard to fully grasp and understand, it is how God has revealed Himself in Scripture. Scripture teaches that the Heavenly Father is God, the Son Jesus Christ is God, and the Holy Spirit is God, and yet there is only one God. (Deuteronomy 6:4; Isaiah 45:5-7; 1 Corinthians 8:4; Galatians 3:20; and 1 Timothy 2:5 convey the existence of only one God.)

Even though Scripture teaches that there is only one God, it also illustrates the plurality (more than one person) in God—not the plurality of God or plurality *outside* of God—**but the plurality *in* God**. For instance, in Genesis 1:26 (author paraphrase), God said: "Let **Us** make man in Our own image after Our own likeness." God the Father, God the Son, and God the Holy Spirit are the "Us" in that verse. All three were involved in the process of creation. This isn't the only verse that demonstrates the plurality in God. Genesis 1:1 (all versions) says: "In the beginning **God** created the heavens and the earth." In that verse, "God" comes from the plural Hebrew noun "*Elohim.*" Elohim is a term used in the Hebrew language to describe the plurality that is in God. We don't know exactly how many persons exist in God from Genesis 1:1 and 26 alone, but throughout the Scriptures, each person of the plurality in God is revealed, identified, and understood as **God the Father, God the Son, and God the Holy Spirit**. In one beautiful passage, we see all three persons of the Trinity at one time. In Matthew 3:16-17, John the Baptist baptizes Jesus (God the Son) in the Jordan River, the Spirit (God the Spirit) descends on Him like a dove, and there's a voice from Heaven from God the Father: "This is my beloved Son, in whom I am well-pleased" (NASB 1995).

Each person of the plurality in God (the Trinity) is God and of the same essence. For instance, the Father isn't any more (or less) God than the Son or Holy Spirit, the Son isn't any more (or less) God than the Father or Holy Spirit, and the Holy Spirit isn't any more (or less) God than the Father and Son. Each person of the plurality in God is equally God and they all coexist eternally. You may have seen a picture like the one below (Figure 1) to illustrate the Trinity.

*Figure 1: The Trinity*

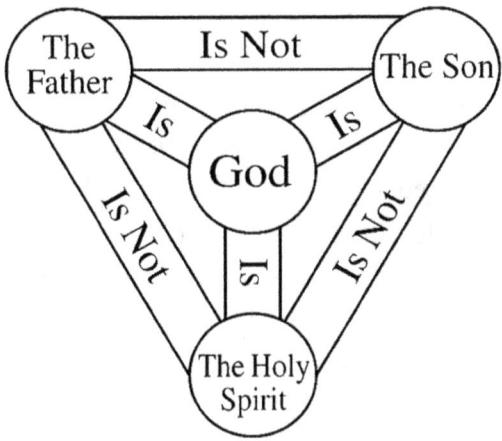

Though all three persons in the Trinity are equally God (as the picture illustrates), each person of the Trinity is yet distinct, and for functional purposes, one person of the Trinity submits to another at varying levels of submission. For example, God the Father predestined the redemption of mankind even before the creation of the world (see Romans 8:29; Ephesians 1:4,5; Revelation 13:8), and Jesus Christ the Son submitted to the will of God the Father to come into the world and die on the cross for our sins (see John 6:38; Philippians 2:5-8) for us to be reconciled back to God and have eternal life with Him. Even though Jesus Christ the Son is equal to God the Father, Jesus did not stick His chest out to ask God the Father: "Why do I have to go down there and die for them? Why can't you go?" Philippians 2:6 affirms that even though Jesus the Son is equal to God the Father, He nevertheless humbled Himself and submitted to the will of God the Father to come into the world and die on the cross for our sins. Also, once Jesus Christ ascended back into Heaven after His resurrection (see Acts 1:9-12), the Holy Spirit submitted to the will of God the Father to come into the world as the Comforter (see John 14:16, 26).

We don't always fully appreciate the fullness of the triune God as the church teaches. God the Father planned and even predestined mankind's redemption (see Ephesians 1:4), God the Son died to pay the price for mankind's redemption by His blood (see Ephesians 1:7), and God the Holy Spirit seals us until the day of redemption (see Ephesians 1:13). God the Father provides for us out of His love, kindness, goodness, grace, mercy, and riches in glory (see Matthew 6:31-32; Philippians 4:19). God the Son sits at the right hand of God the Father to intercede for us (see Romans 8:34). God the Holy Spirit convicts us, comforts us, leads and guides us into all truth (see John 16:13) and empowers us to live a godly life and exemplify God's nature and character (see Galatians 3:29). We can pray to God the Father (see John 14:13), in the Name of God the Son (see John 14:13), in the power of God the Holy Spirit (see Ephesians 6:18).

# CHAPTER 5

# JESUS CHRIST

The virgin birth fascinates and puzzles many people. Some think of the virgin birth as just a myth, while others ponder whether it really happened. I was in my local barbershop once and my barber could not wrap his mind around how the virgin birth could have occurred. In so many words I asked him: "Well, do you believe in miracles?" Miracles do happen (I am a living witness myself) that cannot be explained with natural logic. We consider the virgin birth a miracle, but nothing is too hard for God; there is nothing He cannot do. So why was it necessary that Jesus be born of a virgin, and why did He have to die to save us?

Jesus was (is) known as the God-Man when He walked the earth over two thousand years ago. First Timothy 2:5 says: "For *there is* one God and one Mediator between God and men, *the* Man Christ Jesus, who gave Himself a ransom for all, to be testified in due time." A mediator is a representative of two parties and who also intervenes between two parties to resolve their conflict or bridge the gap between them. Sin, of course, separated mankind from God and destined them to die and go to hell for the penalty or punishment of their sins (Refer to chapter 8). Therefore, God gave us eternal life, pardoned us from the guilt and punishment of our sins, and reconciled us back into fellowship and relationship with Him through His Son Jesus Christ. God sent Jesus into the world to save us from our sins, and that could only be accomplished if Jesus were to be both fully God and fully human. That is why the virgin birth was necessary and significant.

If you're familiar with Greek mythology, you understand that some characters were just considered plain ordinary men (or women), other characters were considered gods (i.e., Zeus, Ares, Athena, Aphrodite, etc.), and yet other characters were half-breeds between humans and gods, or demi-gods (i.e., Hercules, Perseus). Well, that's not Jesus Christ! Jesus was not half god and half man; He was and is 100 percent fully man and 100 percent fully God! Jesus had to be both—the God-Man—to reconcile God and man.

Christ was God's representative, the highest revelation and perfect manifestation of the invisible God (see Colossians 1:15) unto man. At the same time, Christ was also man's representative (intercessor) to God. The concept of Jesus as both fully God (fully divine) and fully man (fully human) extends beyond our human understanding because we tend to think two objects cannot occupy the same space. There are indeed a lot of cults that will deny either the divinity or the humanity of Christ. For instance, several years after the Colossian church was founded, many dangerous false teachings and heresies began to contaminate the church, including "Gnosticism." Gnosticism is derived from the Greek word "*gnosis,*" which means knowledge. Secret knowledge was (is) a significant teaching of Gnosticism. More specifically, the general basis of Gnosticism is that God is good, but all matter is evil. Therefore, Gnostics believe that God would not become human, because He would not dwell in or become a part of matter which is evil, and some secret, higher knowledge beyond Scripture is necessary for one's enlightenment and salvation.

The Apostle Paul refutes this Gnostic heresy by stating: "For in Him [Christ] dwells all the fullness of the Godhead bodily; and you are complete in Him [Christ], who is the head of all principality and power" Colossians 2:9-10. In other words, Paul was saying to the Colossians that Christ possesses all the fullness of the divine nature and attributes of God—Christ was fully divine and fully human. Even the Apostle John refuted Gnosticism in his Gospel writing, arguing for the divinity and incarnation of God in Christ and for God as the Creator. This directly opposed the Gnostic belief that God could not have created all matter (creation) because it was too evil for God to enter into—but the Bible tells us otherwise: "In the beginning was the Word, and the Word was with God, and the Word was God ... All things were made through Him, and without Him nothing was made that was made" (John 1:1, 3), "And the Word became flesh and dwelt among us, and we beheld His glory, the glory as the only begotten of the Father, full of grace and truth" (John 1:14).

## THREE REASONS JESUS HAD TO BE FULLY GOD

Why was (is) it so important for Jesus, our Messiah, to be both divine (fully God) and human (fully man)? Let us begin with Jesus' deity and why that was important.

**Only God Can Forgive and Pardon Sin**

The name of Jesus means "Savior" and "salvation." Joshua in Hebrew is the same name as Jesus in Greek; both mean "salvation." Jesus came into the world as the Messiah, to save the world from their sins (see Matthew 1:21). Only God can forgive sin and offer salvation and justification to mankind, so our Messiah had to be divine (fully God). In Luke 5:21, after Jesus offered to forgive the man for his sins, the Pharisees reasoned and replied: "Who is this who speaks blasphemies? Who can forgive sins but God alone?" No human being has the power or authority to forgive sins, because all sins are an offense against God (see Psalms 51:4). Only God Himself can offer forgiveness of sins and justification. Therefore, it was considered blasphemy for any man to claim he could forgive sin or do what only God can do. The Pharisees were actually right when they asked: "Who can forgive sins but God alone?" However, they were wrong in their assessment of Jesus as a mere man; they failed to realize He was also divine and God incarnate, giving Him the authority to forgive sins.

**Only God Who Is the Source of Life Can Give Life**

A second reason why Jesus our Messiah had to be divine is because no man could offer another man eternal life even if our lives depended on it, as all of us are (were) spiritually dead to begin with. In other words, you cannot give another something you do not have. Therefore, no man could give or offer another man spiritual life (eternal), because our sins rendered us spiritually dead from the beginning. But as God incarnate, Jesus could give eternal life because God is life, the source of life, and the only one who could have offered us life, which is why Jesus said: "I have come that they may have life, and that they may have *it* more abundantly" (John 10:10).

**A Perfect Sacrifice Was Required**

A third reason why Jesus our Messiah had to be divine (fully God) is because a perfect, unblemished sacrifice was required to pay the price for man's sins. Animal sacrifices in the Old Testament were repeatedly offered over and over for a temporary covering (atonement) for the people's sins. Animal sacrifices had to be without spot or blemish, foreshadowing the coming of Jesus Christ who was without sin and would become the perfect sacrifice once and for all (see Romans 6:10; Hebrews 10:10, 12). In that regard, all of us are disqualified, because we all have the spot and blemish of a sinful nature.

## THREE REASONS JESUS HAD TO BE FULLY MAN

Though more could be said on why Jesus our Messiah had to be divine (fully God), let us now consider why it was important for Jesus to be human (fully man).

**The Shedding of Blood Is Required**

The Bible states that the wages of sin is death (see Romans 6:23), so death was the price that had to be paid for sin. Also, without the shedding of blood, there is no remission of sin (see Hebrews 9:22). Remission means to release from the guilt and punishment of sins. Even in the Old Testament, blood always had to be shed (by animal sacrifices); something always had to be killed in place of the sinner for forgiveness (or atonement).

The shedding of blood and death was required to pay the price of mankind's sins. It was therefore important for Jesus our Messiah to become a man (fully human), because God in His infinitely eternal state and glory cannot bleed or die. God needed to become human in the person of Jesus Christ and shed His blood on the cross for our sins.

**The Kinsmen Redeemer**

A second reason why Jesus had to became a man is because of the law of the kinsmen-redeemer (see Genesis 48:16; Exodus 6:6; Leviticus 27:9-25, 25:47-55). No angel could have died to pay for man's sins (nor can God die in His infinitely eternal state and glory). The kinsmen-redeemer was known to be a male relative, who had the privilege of acting on behalf of a relative or family member who was in need, in danger, or in trouble (i.e., Boaz acted as a kinsmen-redeemer when he married Ruth). When Jesus came into the world, as a man, and died on the cross for our sins, He acted as our Kinsmen-Redeemer, to save us from the penalty of our sins.

**To Sympathize with Us**

A third reason Jesus became a man was to identify, relate, and sympathize with us (see Hebrews 4:15). Jesus wept, He slept, He got hungry, and He experienced pain and suffering. Because Jesus lived as a human being, He can relate and sympathize with us. Jesus was also tempted in all things as we are (yet without sin). He knows how we feel; He knows our pain, our struggle, and our heartache. He can feel what we feel, save, help us, and guide us through our human struggles.

## CONCLUSION

To conclude, the virgin birth was essential for Jesus our Messiah to be both fully divine and fully human for salvation from our sins and eternal life. If Mary was impregnated by any man (including Joseph), then the sinful nature passed down from Adam would have been in that child. Without the virgin birth, the child would have been in the same boat as the rest of us—marred and tainted by sin—and unqualified as the perfect sacrifice to pay for our sins. Also, the perfect God cannot bleed or die in His infinite eternal state because He is a Spirit, but without the shedding of blood, there can be no remission for our sins (see Hebrews 9:22). Therefore, Mary had to be impregnated by the Holy Spirit, as a virgin, so that the God-Man Jesus could be the perfect sacrifice and shed His blood for the remission of our sins.

The danger of denying either attribute of Jesus (i.e., human but not divine, divine but not human) is the assumption that the Scriptures and God-ordained prophets of the Bible are inherently wrong about who Jesus is, though they have overwhelmingly conveyed Him as the God-Man and Messiah. Furthermore, it discredits the position of salvation and eternal life through Jesus Christ.

# CHAPTER 6

# THE HOLY SPIRIT

The teaching and ministry of the Holy Spirit is one of the most important things for us to understand from the Scriptures. The work and ministry of the Holy Spirit is evident throughout. Certainly, people may think of the Holy Spirit as some impersonal force or influence or energy, **but the Holy Spirit is an actual person.** Though the Holy Spirit indeed brings power, influence, and energy to a Christian believer, **the Holy Spirit is the very person and presence of God that resides inside every Christian believer.** Therefore, a believer should be careful not to think of the Holy Spirit as merely an impersonal force or influence, lest it robs him of the opportunity to have a personal relationship and communion with Him.

The Holy Spirit is revealed in Scripture to be the third person of the Trinity (see 1 John 5:7). The Holy Spirit is also referenced with personal pronouns. Though "Spirit" is not technically associated with gender, Jesus used personal pronouns such as

"He," "Him," and "Himself" when referring to the Holy Spirit (see John 14:15, 16, 26; 16:7-14; 15:26-27). The Holy Spirit hears and speaks (see John 16:13), can grieve (see Ephesians 4:30), and is also described as having a mind (see Romans 8:27), a will (see 1 Corinthians 12:11), and emotions (see Romans 8:26-27). An impersonal force would not have any of these traits.

The Holy Spirit is also known as the "Comforter" which means "Helper" or "Advocate" (see John 14:16, 26; 15:26; 16:7) who stands alongside us. As Jesus made it aware to His disciples that we would soon be leaving them (via His death, burial, resurrection, and ascension), He promised that He would not leave them comfortless, but the Father would send them another comforter (the Holy Spirit), in His place (see John 14:15-17, 25-26). **Therefore, the Holy Spirit would come to be the personal presence and comfort of God inside of them, even as Jesus was to them when He walked the earth.**

# CHAPTER 7

# ANGELS AND DEMONS

Though not eternal like God, angels are spirit beings created by God (see Psalms 148:1-5; Colossians 1:16) who are also immortal and part of the unseen, spiritual world (see Luke 20:34-36). Angels shouted for joy as they witnessed God's creation of the world (see Job 38:4-7). Angels have intelligence, will, personality, and emotions (see Genesis 16:7-12; 19:1-17; Judges 13:1-21; Matthew 8:9). Angels appear to have wisdom, knowledge, and strength that is superior to mankind's for the following reasons:

1) Angels are a higher order of creation than man, as the Bible says man was created "a little lower than the angels" (Psalms 8:5, KJV).
2) Angels have existed for at least as long as the world itself (and probably longer) as they witnessed God's creation (see Job 38:4-7), which means they have existed for thousands of

years at minimum. Naturally, their wisdom and knowledge would increase throughout the ages, though they are not omniscient (all-knowing) like God (see Matthew 24:36).

3) Angels are not limited by space or time, at least not to the extent that man is. Though angels can only be in one place at one time (see Job 1:6; Daniel 10:12-14), they can move (fly) at a speed or means beyond what we know or understand (see Daniel 9:21). Perhaps they can move a million times faster than the speed of light or simply teleport by the very thought.

The Bible says that when the poor man died, the angels immediately carried (transferred) him into Abraham's bosom (see Luke 16:22). It appears that angels can travel immediately from earth to heaven (see Job 1:6) or from heaven to earth (see Revelation 20:1).

4) The strength and power of angels are conveyed in the following Scriptures: Psalms 103:20, 2 Kings 19:35; 2 Peter 2:11; 2 Thessalonians 1:7; and Revelation 18:1, 21. For instance, one angel killed 185,000 Assyrians in defense of King Hezekiah and the Kingdom of Judah (2 Kings 19:35). Angels have strength and power beyond man though they are not all-powerful or all-mighty (omnipotent) like God.

As men (and women), we are created "a little lower than angels" (Psalms 8:5, KJV) because we are not yet immortal like they are nor as strong as they are, nor do we have wisdom and knowledge to their extent. We are also more prone to fallibility, sin, and corruption than good angels are, and we also don't have direct access (yet) to the heavenly presence of God-like angels. Flesh and blood cannot bear the presence of the full glory of God;

which is why Christian believers will have new glorious and spiritual bodies to inhabit at the resurrection (see 1 Corinthians 15). However, as men, we relate to God in such a way that angels cannot; we have a most peculiar, distinct, and incomparable relationship with God that angels cannot know; we have a certain connection and experience with God that angels can never have nor experience, and that relationship is through the grace and redemption of Jesus Christ. Angels can never know the grace given to us through the blood and sacrifice of Jesus Christ because they are immortal and do not suffer from the curse of degeneration, sin, and death as man does.

## GOOD ANGELS

Good angels are known to be God's holy or elect angels (see 1 Timothy 5:21) whose ministry primarily involves obeying, serving, praising and worshipping God (see Psalms 91:11, 148:2; Daniel 7:9-10; Matthew 28:53; Luke 2:13; Hebrews 12:22; Revelation 5:11). At times, God will send His good angels as heavenly messengers to encourage and affirm His Word, His will, or His promises to mankind (see Genesis 16:9, 18:1-15; Judges 6:1-22, 13:2-22; Daniel 10:12-14; Matthew 1:20-24; Luke 1:11-20, 26-38). Good angels also guide the righteous (see Genesis 24:7; Exodus 23:20), protect the righteous (see Psalms 34:7, 2 Kings 19:35), serve and help the righteous (1 Kings 19:5), carry out divine commands given by God and His judgment upon people or nations (see Genesis 19, 2 Samuel 24:16, 1 Chronicles 21:15, Revelation 8-22).

Even though angels are spirits, they have been shown to transform or take on human form and flesh throughout Scripture (see

Genesis 18:2, 19, 32:25-30; Judges 6:11-22, 13:3-21). Hebrews 13:2 says: "Be not forgetful to entertain [or show hospitality to] strangers: for thereby some have entertained [or have shown hospitality] angels unawares" (KJV). Hebrews encourages us to show hospitality even to strangers because they could be angels sent by God to communicate a message or affirm His Word with a promise to us. He may send angels to test how we treat them, which is what happened with Samson's father. He wasn't aware at first that the man was an angel of God sent to him and his wife to prophesy their child's (Samson) birth and purpose—delivering the Israelites (see Judges 13:3-21).

Good angels are ministering spirits (see Hebrews 1:7) and can appear in both human and non-human forms. Scripture reveals the appearances and disappearances of angels as evidence of their immortality. An angel disappears in Judges 6:21; an angel ascends in the flame of an altar in Judges 13:20; an angel appears as lightning in dazzling clothing white as snow in Matthew 28:3; and an angel whose body is like beryl, face like lighting, eyes like flaming torches, and arms and feet like polished bronze appears in Daniel 10:5-6. Angels can *also* transform and take on human form or flesh as inconspicuous or ordinary human beings. Through Scripture, angels have typically taken on the male human form. For example, the Bible refers to the angel as a "man" or a "he" in Genesis 18:2, 19, 32:25-30, Judges 6:13, 13:3-21; 2 Kings 1:6; 1 Chronicles 21:15; Matthew 28:3; Luke 1:28; and Revelation 12:7.

I recall a dramatic encounter that my mother and I had with angels in 2005! Our home church was located in Fort Mill, SC, but on this day, we traveled to Greenville for a youth program.

I lived about thirty minutes away from Greenville at the time. When we arrived in Greenville, we went through an intersection with a green traffic light, and suddenly, at full speed, a man ran the red light at the intersection's crossroad. His car plowed right into us and spun from the impact. Our car slid off the road, the airbags blew out, smoke erupted, and the car was totaled. All of that happened so fast, in the blink of an eye. Miraculously, my mother and I walked away from that collision with no scars, bruises, or soreness—and a car that was totaled—because of God's divine intervention and protection. His angels were encamped about us that day, and although I didn't visually see the angels, we know they were there and protected us!

After the accident, my mother and I were thinking about getting checked out at the doctor, but we decided to go to church first. There were many churches on that street, so we went to the wrong one the first time, but God had a purpose for it. The pastor of that church, a lady, met us and prayed for me and my mother. I really felt the power of God moving and flowing as she prayed and prophesized, and I just broke into tears. I knew God was using her to speak, as she said: "The devil tried to take you out of here tonight, but said God no! He had his guardian angels encamped about you! And the reason why hell has broken loose on your life is because you are anointed.... you have a calling on your life, and when you speak that word, speak it boldly!" She also told my mother: "Mother, you're blessed, you're blessed." I always knew in my heart that God had bestowed upon me His calling and anointing for preaching and declaring His word, and that day, my calling and what had happened was confirmed prophetically.

## BAD ANGELS

Evil or fallen angels (2 Peter 2;4; Jude 6, 9) are known to be demons and accomplices of Satan (2 Timothy 4:1). Satan is known to be the enemy and adversary of God and mankind and leader of the fallen angels. Satan was formally known as the angel called Lucifer, the prince of the morning (see Isaiah 14:12). Lucifer possessed indescribable brightness, glory, and beauty before he rebelled against God (see Ezekiel 28:12-13). He was also full of wisdom (see Ezekiel 28:12) and blameless from the day that God created him (see Ezekiel 28:15). Like a cherub, he was closest to the throne of God (see Ezekiel 28:14) and could have very well been the bishop (overseer) of the heavenly praise and worship (see Ezekiel 28:13).

Yet, Lucifer's beauty, glory, and pride corrupted him. He wanted to exalt himself above all the other angels in heaven to be like God (see Isaiah 14:13-14). He managed to entice a third of the angelic host in rebellion against God and against the holy angels (see Revelation 12:7-9). As a result, Lucifer and his angels were thrown out of heaven by force (see Revelation 12:9) and irrevocably sentenced to burn in everlasting hell fire (see Matthew 25:41). Hell was created originally for Lucifer and his angels (see Matthew 25:41) after their rebellion against God. Lucifer is known as Satan and the devil in his fallen state (see 1 Peter 5:8), the ruler of demons (see Matthew 9:34; Mark 3:22), the great deceiver of the world (see Revelation 12:9), the father of lies (see John 8:44), the prince of the powers of the air (see Ephesians 2:2), the adversary (see 1 Peter 5:8), the accuser (see Psalms 109:6; Revelation 12:10), the prowling lion (see 1 Peter

5:8) who seeks to devour, and the one who comes to steal, kill, and destroy (see John 10:10).

Since the time that Lucifer indulged in his pride to exalt himself as God and was thrown of out heaven by force, he has attacked, fought, and sought to vandalize God's most prized and cherished creation—us, whom God has made in His image and after His likeness. Satan has always attempted to destroy mankind who are reflections of God's glory and bear His image in order to get back at God. **Therefore, Satan is mankind's enemy because he was God's enemy first, from the moment that pride led him to rebel against God. Satan is mankind's greatest enemy and foe; he is the greatest risk and threat to your soul, and you must be aware of him!**

It's also important to recognize that while Satan is our enemy and God's enemy, he **is not God's** equal, because **God has no equal!** Satan is a created being. God didn't create Satan to be Satan; God created Lucifer in perfection and blamelessness (see Ezekiel 28:15), yet Lucifer, as a result of his own pride and self-will to be like God, was kicked out of heaven (see Isaiah 14:12-15) and became Satan (see Job 1:7). You may ask, "If God is all-powerful, all-mighty, all-seeing, and all-knowing," (and He is), "why didn't He prevent or stop Lucifer/Satan from rebelling against Him?" Yes, God could have stopped his rebellion and at any moment destroyed or annihilated him just by thinking about it, saying "zap!", or snapping His finger. We may never come to understand why God allowed Lucifer/Satan to rebel against Him and/or why He hasn't destroyed Lucifer/Satan yet, but what is certain is that God has appointed a time for Satan and his angels (demons) to be fully destroyed in the lake of fire (see Matthew 25:41; Revelation 20:10). For thousands of years since the creation of the world,

Satan and his demons have roamed the earth and will continue to do so until their appointed time—so we must be aware!

Though we can't see Satan or demons with our physical eyes because they are spirits and part of the unseen spiritual world, we can clearly see their effects in the physical world. Their person, their presence, and their activity are just as real in the physical world as the things we see, hear, taste, touch, and smell. To arm your soul against them, you must first be aware of their existence and activity! Satanic (demonic) activity is very real and at work in the world and in people's lives today. John 10:10 gives a good summary of what Satan and his demons do: "The thief comes not but for to steal, to kill and to destroy" (author paraphrase). Satan and his demonic spirits seek to attack and oppress mankind spiritually, emotionally, morally, mentally, and even physically. Satan leads many different kinds of demons and evil spirits (see Table 2). Throughout the Scriptures, you'll often find their activity exposes their very nature.

## TABLE 2: THE DIFFERENT NAMES AND NATURE OF DEMONS

| NAME | NATURE | SCRIPTURE |
| --- | --- | --- |
| Evil Spirits | Speaks of the evil or ill will demons possess towards mankind | Luke 7:21 |
| Unclean Spirits | Induces impurity and wickedness in a person | Matthew 10:1, 12:43 |

| | | |
|---|---|---|
| Dumb Spirits | Mutes or curses a person with inability to speak | Mark 9:17, Luke 11:14 |
| Blind Spirits | Induces blindness in a person | Matthew 12:22 |
| Deaf Spirits | Induces deafness in a person | Mark 9:25 |
| Spirit of Infirmity | Causes ailment | Luke 13:11 |
| Seducing Spirits | Seduces people away from the truth and faith of God | 1 Timothy 4:1 |
| Epileptic Spirits | Induces epilepsy and suicidal tendencies | Matthew 17:15-18 |
| Distressing Spirits | Seeks to trouble and bring distress | 1 Samuel 16:14 |
| Oppressing Spirits | Seeks to oppress, exercise control, and overburden. | Acts 10:38 |
| Tormenting/Vexing Spirits | Seeks to bring torment and/or vexing sensations, impressions, feelings (pain) to a person. | Acts 5:16 |

Even though Satan has supernatural power, he cannot duplicate or recreate what God does; Satan can only try to imitate or counterfeit what God does. In fact, this is his favorite method for deceiving and leading people astray from God. The Bible says that Satan disguises himself as an angel of light (see 2 Corinthians 11:14). A lot of supernatural activity occurs in the spirit realm and there are numerous satanic means of invoking the supernatural and even communicating with the spirit realm through the occultic arts and spiritism. The actual word occult means "to hide," "hidden," or "concealed things." Occult arts and practices are counterfeit means that Satan and his demons use to deceive and distance people from God. God has provided a way for man to know Him, mainly through His Word, through Jesus Christ, and through the Holy Spirit. When man rejects God's invitation to know Him in those ways, man then becomes vulnerable to Satan and his counterfeit work, and Satan fulfills his purpose—to keep man enslaved. It's the reason why the Bible gives strong warnings about the consequences of participating in occultic arts and practices (see Leviticus 19:31, 20:6; Deuteronomy 18:10). Genuine miracles are signs that point people to God and cause them to believe, whereas Satan's counterfeit signs, counterfeit wonders, and counterfeit miracles are designed to deceive people, pull them away from God, and keep them in bondage (see Revelation 13:12). Therefore, Satan and His demons pose as a threat against your very life and soul (see John 10:10; 1 Peter 5:8). **Protection and security and victory against these dark, evil spiritual forces can only be found in God** (see 2 Corinthians 10:4; Ephesians 6:11-18).

Spirits can be tested in the light of God's Word (see Isaiah 8:19-20), in the light of the truth about Jesus Christ (see 1 John 4:2-3), and by the discernment of Holy Spirit (see 1 Corinthians

12:7-10; Acts 16:16-18). Furthermore, Jesus was victorious in crushing the power of Satan and his demons when He died on the cross for our sins and was raised again from the dead (see Ephesians 4:8; Colossians 2:15). Even when Jesus Christ walked the earth over 2,000 years ago, every demon including Satan was subject to the power and authority and Word of Jesus Christ (see Matthew 8:31-32, 17:18; Mark 5:12, 9:25-26; Luke 9:42). **Because of this, our souls can be devil proof!** We can live and walk in victory over Satan and his demons by the power, authority, victory, and means God has provided for us in Jesus Christ (see Luke 10:17-20; Romans 8:28-39; 1 Corinthians 15:57; 2 Corinthians 10:4; Ephesians 6:11-18)!

Yet Satan (and his demons) are not the only threats against your life and your very soul. Two other great threats are **the flesh** and **the world**.

There are three specific threats/enemies that you need to be aware of:

1) The devil (Satan and his demons)
2) The flesh
3) The world

## The Flesh

The word "flesh" in the Bible is not necessarily a reference to the soft tissue consisting of muscles and fat that's found between our skin and bones, but a reference to our inherent sinful human nature, our inherent capacity to sin. Our sinful human nature (our flesh) has an inherent desire (lust) to rebel against God and indulge in sin. The Apostle Paul says, "The flesh lusts against the Spirit, and the Spirit against the flesh . . . so that you would not do the things that you wish (Galatians 5:17). Without the Spirit of God in our lives, we all have a disposition towards sin. Even a Christian who has a relationship with God, loves God, desires to please God, and desires to walk in God's will and God's ways will yet feel this internal conflict and struggle between the flesh and the Holy Spirit (see Romans 7:14-25; Galatians 5:17). The good news is that Christians don't have to yield to the lust and sins of our flesh when we yield to the power and leading of the Holy Spirit and God's Word.

## The World

There are three ways that "world" is used in the Bible:
1) The physical, material world (see Romans 1:20; Hebrews 11:3).
2) The human race (see John 3:16).
3) The satanic world system in opposition against God (see Romans 12:2; 2 Corinthians 4:4; 1 John 2:15-16).

The Apostle John uses it to refer to the satanic system: "Love not the world, neither the things *that are* in the world. If any man love the world, the love of the Father is not in him. For all that *is* in the world, **the lust of the flesh, and the lust of the eyes, and the pride of life**, is not of the Father, but is of the world" (1 John 2:15-17, KJV).

**PART 2**

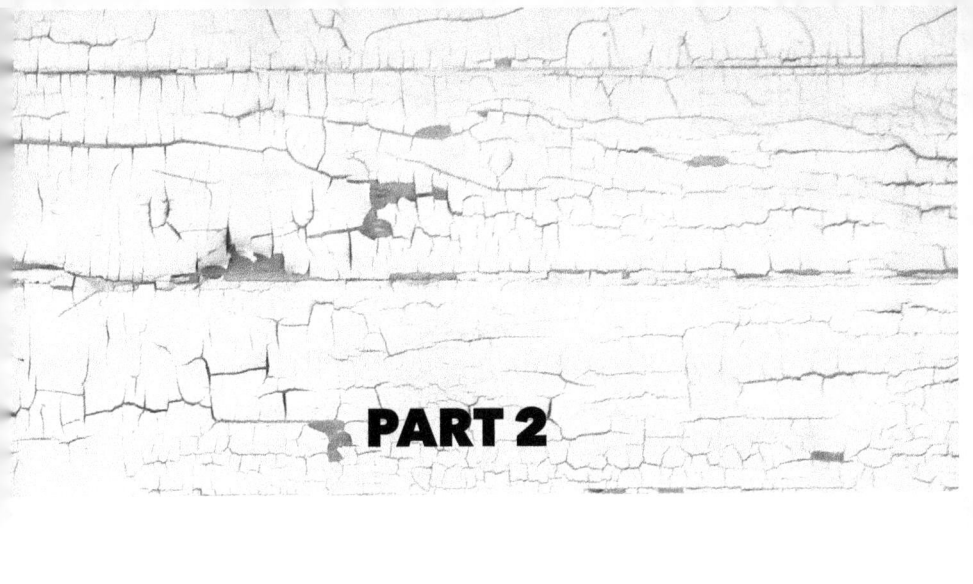

# UNDERSTANDING THE CONDITION OF YOUR SOUL

# CHAPTER 8

# THE ULTIMATE BAD NEWS, GOOD NEWS SCENARIO

We have all had someone give us a bad news good news scenario: "Guess what? I have good news and bad news; which do you want to hear first?" Many of us tend to choose the bad news first because we are generally more attentive to and alarmed by bad news than good news. When people give me a choice between hearing the good news or bad news first, I choose to hear the bad news first, because I always like to hear a good ending.

Of course, bad news tends to dominate the news broadcast and make headlines. Whether or not we keep up with what is happening in the world around us, we all know there is a lot of bad news: sickness, diseases, chaos, confusion, degeneration, corruption, evil, wickedness, calamity, suffering, crying, pain, killings, murders, crime, war, natural disasters, death, etc. Why do all these things occur in our world today? With all these things happening, we can certainly use some good news! The Gospel literally means "good news." The Gospel is God's good news for you (and for me)! If God has good news for us, then bad news must also exist. So what is the bad news? What is the ultimate good news bad news scenario?

The Bible says that God created everything for His own pleasure (see Revelation 4:11); all of creation is an awesome display of God's love, power, and creativity (see Romans 1:20). During the first five days of creation, God created the heavens and the earth (see Genesis 1:1); He formed the infinitely vast universe with innumerable galaxies, stars, and planets (the second heaven). He created the earth with seas, dry land, trees, fruit, vegetation, and all the animals and creatures (see Genesis 1:1-31), but on the sixth day of creation, God made His most prized and precious creation when He said: "Let Us make man in Our own image, after Our own likeness" (Genesis 1:26, author paraphrase).

God created you and made you in His image because He desired a living being whom He could have fellowship and a relationship with. God desired man to express His love and goodness. As people made in God's image, we have the capacity of free will to communicate and reciprocate love back to God. When God said: "Let Us make man," He was referring to the Trinity of Himself (Heavenly Father), His Son (Jesus Christ), and the Holy Spirit. Being made in God's image, after His likeness, means that God created us to represent Him and resemble Him. Being made in God's image and likeness, we are not God, nor are we equal to God (and will never be), but we are representations of God who resemble God (i.e., His glory, His nature, His communicable traits and attributes) in the functional sense. For instance, because we are made in God's image and likeness, we have intelligence and intellect; we have the capacity to think, to reason, to rationalize, to choose, to show emotion, and we are moral agents.

In contrast, animals are not intelligent; they cannot rationalize, reason, or show emotion (a dog will not smile or frown at you). They are not moral agents but only act and react by their natural instincts.

Being made in God's image and likeness, we can also commune with God our Creator (because we have a soul/spirit). We have the capacity to love and show kindness and goodness (God's communicable attributes). Also, just as God the Father, God the Son, and God the Holy Spirit are in fellowship and relationship with each other, we are also relational beings because we were made and created in the image of the Triune God. However, herein lies the bad news. There was something that broke mankind's fellowship and relationship with God. The Garden of Eden was pure bliss for Adam and Eve. They had everything they could ever need and want; they walked and talked with God in perfect fellowship and relationship with Him until something bad and tragic happened that separated Adam and Eve from God. What is it that breaks our fellowship and relationship with God? Sin. Sin is what separated Adam and Eve from God.

When God originally created the world, He made everything good. Genesis 1:31 (NASB) says: "God saw all that He had made, and behold, it was very good." If everything was once very good, how did things get very bad in our world today? Why in the world do we have and witness and experience such things as sickness, diseases, chaos, confusion, degeneration, corruption, evil, wickedness, calamity, suffering, crying, pain, crime, war, guilt, fear, shame, and death? All of these things originate from one big problem. What is the one big problem with our world (and with us) today? **It is sin!** Romans 5:12 (KJV) says: "Wherefore, as by one man [Adam] sin entered into the world, and death by sin; and so death passed upon all men, for that all have sinned." When God originally created the world, it was indeed very good; there was no suffering, no pain, no crying, no sadness, no cannibalism (i.e., animals eating and ripping each other apart), no sorrow, no crime, no war, no sickness, no diseases, no death. It was only after Adam (and Eve) sinned that everything went from being very good to very bad. The nature and curse of sin were passed on to all of creation and the entire human race. What we have is a sin problem. Table 3 denotes how the world was before and after the curse of sin.

| THE WORLD BEFORE AND AFTER SIN ||
|---|---|
| **The World Before Sin** (God Created Everything Good; Genesis 1:31) | **The Curse and Effects of Sin** (When Sin Entered the World Through Adam (Romans 5:12) |
| No death, morning, sadness, crying, pain, sickness, disease, suffering, crime, war, evil, wickedness, or calamity. This condition will once again exist in heaven (Revelation 21:4). | Death, morning, sadness, crying, pain, sickness, disease, suffering, crime, war, evil, wickedness, and calamity. |

| | |
|---|---|
| No degeneration (corruption). | Degeneration (corruption): The physical world around us goes towards disorder, decay/degeneration. This is the Law of Entropy in thermodynamics where physical matter will continually decay, disintegrate, and break down to disorder. |
| No natural disasters | Hurricanes, earthquakes, tornadoes, hailstorms, etc. |
| No cannibals (Animals and even dinosaurs did not eat each other, nor was any animal a threat to humans because every animal was originally created to be herbivores (Genesis 1:30). Animals and humans did not fear each other. During the millennial reign of Christ, this condition will be once again be restored on earth (Isaiah 65:25). | Some animals are wild and cannibalistic; they hunt and eat other animals. Humans also fear wild animals and animals fear humans. |

Just like a hereditary disease or disorder that is passed down from a parent and inherited by the child(ren), the condition and disorder of sin were also passed down from Adam and inherited by the offspring of the entire human race (along with all of creation). Everyone who has ever been born after Adam bears the same sinful nature and curse of death. You may ask, "How can we be held accountable and considered guilty for what Adam did thousands upon thousands of years ago in the Garden of Eden?" You may think it isn't fair or right for God to judge us for Adam's sin. However, when Adam sinned, his propensity to sin (sinful nature), like a hereditary disease, was passed down to his offspring (the entire human race).

One definition of sin in Greek means to "miss the mark." If you've ever played darts before, you know that you must aim and throw your darts to hit the mark of the bull's eye. God has a mark (see Figure 2), a standard for mankind to aim for and live by—His Holy law and character (the Bible).

*Figure 2: The Mark God Desires Mankind to Aim for*

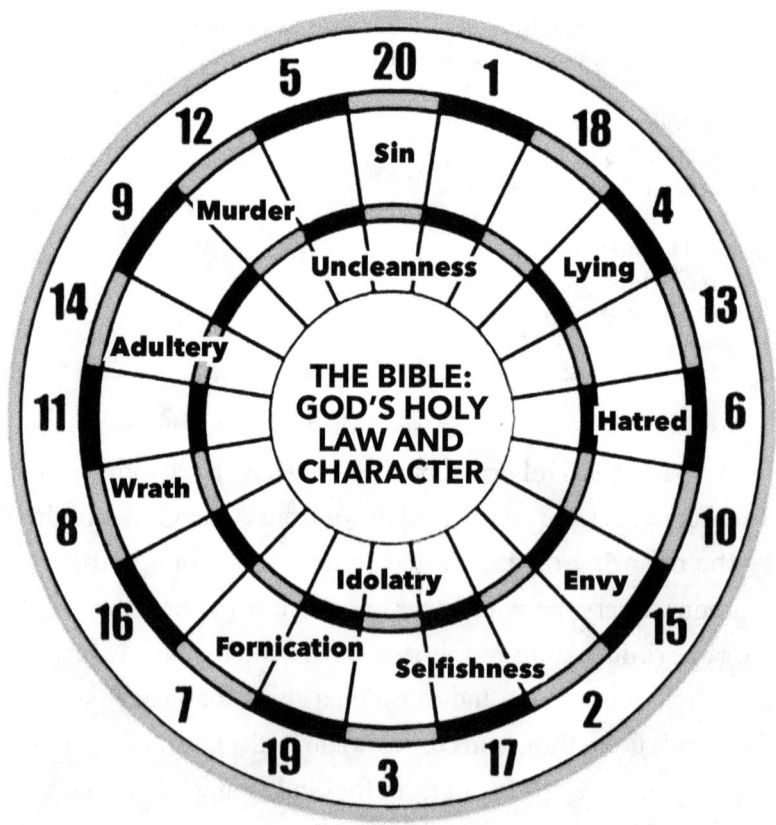

Sin shows up whenever mankind fails, comes up short, or "misses the mark" of living to the standard of God's Holy law and character. We can sin against God in three ways:
1) By our thoughts
2) By our words
3) By our actions

Also, the two types of sins are:

1) **Sins of Commission:** A sin that we take the initiative to commit (intentionally or unintentionally) with our thoughts, words, and/or actions.

2) **Sins of Omission:** A sin where we refuse (omit) to do what we know to be good or right.

Our sins confirm our fallen nature that is of Adam; we are not sinners because we sin, we sin because we are sinners. But herein lies the good news (the Gospel)! The good news is that despite man's fall and separation (death), God provided the means to reverse the curse and effects of sin and redeem man back to Himself. This is the ultimate good news bad news scenario. The ultimate bad news is that sin separated mankind from God and the wages (punishment) for sin is death (physical death and ultimately spiritual/eternal death), but the ultimate good news is God loved us too much not to provide a way to redeem mankind (you and me) back to Himself in fellowship and relationship.

## GOD'S PROVISION FOR OUR CONDITION

God desires to have fellowship and relationship with us; it was for this purpose that He made us and created us in His image. But since sin has tainted mankind and mankind is, by default, separated from God, God purposed us to be saved (redeemed) in order to have fellowship and relationship with Him. What does that mean to be saved? Saved from what? A person is saved from the penalty and punishment of their sins (death) as a result of confessing their sins and accepting Jesus Christ as their personal Lord and Savior (see Romans 10:9) and believing in who He is and what He did to pay the price for our sins through His death, burial, and resurrection.

God has made it possible for any and every person who desires fellowship and relationship with Him to have them through Jesus Christ. **Being redeemed back to God through Jesus Christ is the ultimate protection and security of our soul,** but it is always a person's choice. Did you know that God's original reason and intention for creating hell, the place of fiery torment and suffering, was for Satan and his demons (see Matthew 18:9)? God did not originally create hell for human beings. However, if a person refuses or chooses not to have fellowship and a relationship with God, He will allow or permit that person to go to hell, because hell is the place that defines all that it means to be without God (without His presence, without His fellowship and relationship, without His goodness, without His comfort, without His peace, without His grace, without His mercy, without His love, and without His kindness). In contrast, heaven is the place that ultimately defines everything it means to be with God (in His presence, His fellowship and relationship, His blessings, goodness, comfort, peace, joy, grace, mercy, love, and kindness).

You hear people ask, "How could a loving, merciful God send a person to hell?" God does not send anyone to hell, nor does He desire for any person to go to hell; that is why He has already made a way for us to have fellowship and a relationship with Him through Jesus Christ. He has prepared heaven for anyone who desires eternal fellowship and a relationship with Him. Any person who goes to hell will go there by their own choice because they refused God. Though God is sovereign, all-mighty, and all-powerful, He will never impose His will on us. God created us with free will to choose whether we want to have fellowship and a relationship with Him or not.

Whenever we hear a bad news, good news scenario, the next question we always ponder is: "What are you going to do about it? Now that I know what the bad news and good news are, what am I going to do with the news I've just heard?" In a bad news good news scenario, the bad news is often the way things already are, and the good news is the solution to change the way things are for the better. For instance, suppose a doctor comes to you and says: "I have bad news and good news, which do you want to hear first? You say: "Bad news first please." And the doctor replies: "Well the bad news is you have high cholesterol and are at high risk for a heart attack if your cholesterol does not go down, but the good news is you can lower your cholesterol and risk for a heart attack with proper dieting and exercise." Would you just walk away and do nothing with the doctor's solution, or would you put the good news to use to change your situation (the bad news)? Now, consider the ultimate bad news, good news scenario for you. What would you do with the good news?

Table 4 lays out the nuances of the bad news, good news scenarios.

| TABLE 4: **THE ULTIMATE BAD NEWS, GOOD NEWS SCENARIOS** | | |
|---|---|---|
| REALMS | THE BAD NEWS | THE GOOD NEWS |
| Relational Realm | Sin broke mankind's fellowship and relationship with God and the wages (penalty) for our sins is death (Romans 5:12, 6:23). | God loved us so much that He sent His one and only divine son Jesus Christ to die in our place to pay for the penalty of our sins, to reconcile us back in fellowship and relationship with Him, and have eternal life with Him (John 3:16, Romans 6:23). |
| Physical Realm | We experience, death, sickness, diseases, pain, suffering, crying, evil, wickedness, chaos, confusion, crime, war, etc. in our world as a result of the curse of sin. The physical world continually wears down, decays, disintegrates, and breaks down to disorder (Law of Entropy) (Psalms 102:25-26, Isaiah 51:6). | Jesus came to reverse the curse and effects of sin; through Christ, neither sin nor the curse/effects of sin have dominion over us. All of creation, everything in the physical universe will ultimately be renewed from the curse and effects of sin (Romans 8:19, Revelation 21:4). |

# THE ULTIMATE BAD NEWS, GOOD NEWS SCENARIO

| | | |
|---|---|---|
| Animal Realm | Some animals are wild and cannibalistic to hunt down and prey on other animals for food. Humans fear certain (wild) animals, some animals also fear humans (Psalm 104:19-21). | The time will once again come when the wolf dwells of the lamb, the lion will eat straw like an ox, and dust for the serpent's food (Isaiah 65:25). The known dangers from the animal world will not exist during the 1000-year (Millennial) Reign of Christ on the earth (Isaiah 65:17, Revelation 20:4). |
| Spirit Realm | Satan and his demons wage war against God by waging war against those made and created in God's image (you and I). Therefore, Satan and his demons will be restless and active in this world and in our own lives to wreak havoc (Luke 22:31-34, 1 Peter 5:8). | Satan, his demons, and their power have already been conquered and defeated by the death, burial, and resurrection of Jesus Christ. God has provided the spiritual armor and weaponry (2 Corinthians 10:4; Ephesians 6:11-18) we need through Christ, in order to stand, to triumph, and to be victorious over the schemes and tactics of Satan and his demons. |
| Hell Realm | Though God originally created hell for Satan and his demons, if you choose not to have fellowship and a relationship with *(cont'd on next page)* | God loved you so much, He provided the means through Jesus Christ, in order for you to have fellowship and a relationship with Him, *(cont'd on next page)* |

| | | |
|---|---|---|
| Hell Realm, cont. | God and end up dying with that choice, hell will be the place you will spend eternity (in fire and torment) (Matthew 25:41). | along with eternal life, and the unspeakable joy of heaven (Revelation 21-22). |
| Death Realm | Sin produced death (separation). Physical death is when the soul separates from the body; spiritual death is being separated from God, and eternal death is to be eternally, permanently separated from God (Genesis 2:17, Romans 5:12, 6:23). | Because Christ was risen from the dead, He conquered and defeated death. In Christ, death's power and sting have been removed and have no dominion over those who are in Christ. Those who are in Christ have life and victory over death (Romans 8:37, 1 Corinthians 15:50-57, 2 Corinthians 2:14, 1 John 5:11-12). |

# PART 3

# KNOWING GOD PERSONALLY: MAKING YOUR SOUL SECURE IN GOD

# CHAPTER 9

# YOUR SECRET ADMIRER!

A secret admirer adores, is fond of, or even loves another person who is unaware of the affection. When I was around eleven or twelve years old, I was just blown away by this young, beautiful, and intelligent lady. Every time I saw her—I mean every time—it felt like my heart was beating out of my chest. I liked her but she had no idea that I felt that way about her, so for a while, I was her secret admirer. I would drop off boxes of Little Debbie cakes on her front porch and then knock on the front door and run away. I even wrote her a poem one time. One line read: "You're the sugar to my Kool-Aid!" I would imagine she was wondering, "Who in the world is this boy who thinks I'm the sugar to his Kool-Aid!?!"

Did you know that the God and Creator of the entire universe desires to make Himself known through personal fellowship and relationship with you!? In a sense, God is your secret admirer, because long before you ever thought about God, God had you in mind and was thinking about you! Long before you were even born and the world was ever created, God predetermined to set His love, affection, and special regard upon you with a great purpose and plan for your life! The Bible says that God created everything for His own pleasure (see Revelation 4:11). All of creation is an awesome display of God's love, power, and creativity. More specifically, God created you and made you in His image because He desired a living person with whom He could have fellowship and a relationship. **Because God desires to have fellowship and a relationship with us, He desires for us to know Him! The unknown God (see Acts 17:23) can be known and wants to be known by you!** How can you come to know God?

# CHAPTER 10

# KNOWING GOD THROUGH FAITH

The way we come to know God first and initially is through faith. The Bible defines faith for us in Hebrews 11:1. It says: "Now faith is the substance of things hoped for, the evidence of things not seen" (KJV). The NIRV version says: "Faith is being sure of what we hope for. It is being sure of what we do not see." My mother raised my younger sister, my older brother, and me as a single parent. She took care of us, but I remember as a little boy my grandfather would sometimes help my mother in many ways, like buying groceries and other kind and generous things. When my mother told us that grandfather was coming by with groceries, I often leaped for joy because I was always happy to see him and happy to have some groceries, too! But as soon as my mother would say: "Your grandfather is coming by!" I always believed and trusted grandfather would come by, no matter how long it would take for him to arrive—and he always did!

The Bible says that God is a Spirit (see Chapter 3) and no man has physically seen God (see John 1:18). Therefore, faith is the one thing that God requires for us to know Him, as the Bible says: "Without faith *it is* impossible to please *Him*; for he who comes to God must believe that He is, and *that* He is a rewarder of those who diligently seek Him" (Hebrews 11:6). We must first **BELIEVE** and **TRUST** that God is, as there is clear evidence of God's existence and power (see Chapter 2). We must **BELIEVE** and **TRUST** that He rewards those who seek Him, those who put forth a sincere, genuine effort into seeking God. This same verse also affirms that God desires to know us, as He rewards those who diligently seek to know Him and who will come to Him in faith (see Hebrews 11:6; James 4:8). If you draw near (seek) after God, God will draw near to you (see James 4:8).

# CHAPTER 11

# KNOWING GOD THROUGH JESUS CHRIST

Believing that God is (that He exists) is what I would call "initial faith." Yet coming to know God through a redemptive (saved from the punishment of our sins) relationship requires "saving faith." "Initial faith" alone is not "saving faith." "Saving faith" involves BELIEF and TRUST in the One whom God the Heavenly Father has sent to die on the cross for our sins—Jesus Christ, the Son of God (see John 3:16). On another occasion, Jesus Himself said, "the work of God is this: to believe in the One He has sent" (see John 6:29, NIV). Jesus Christ is the full expression and complete revelation of the invisible God as Colossians 1:15 says: "He (Jesus Christ) is the image of the invisible God, the firstborn over all creation." Jesus also tells His disciples on another occasion: "I am the way, the truth, and the life. No one comes to the Father except through Me. If you had known Me, you would have known My Father also; and from now on you know Him and have seen Him" (John 14:6-7). Therefore, we cannot come to know God apart from His Son Jesus Christ. We enter a redemptive relationship with God the Heavenly Father by His Son Jesus Christ in two ways:

1) **Through faith in Jesus Christ:** Ephesians 2:8-9 (author paraphrase) says: "We are saved by grace through faith in Jesus Christ and not by our own effort or works." In other words, we cannot be saved based on our own efforts, merit, or works; it is only by faith in Jesus Christ and in Jesus Christ alone that we are saved from the punishment of our sins which is death (see Romans 6:23). Faith in Jesus Christ involves:
    - Believing that Jesus Christ is who the Bible says He is (see John 6:29).
    - Believing in the facts recorded in the Bible about Jesus Christ, such as: He is the Son of God (see John 3:16), He is God who became flesh when He walked the earth nearly 2,000 years ago (see John 1:1, 14), He is Lord and Messiah (Savior) (see Philippians 2:10), He died on the cross to save you from your sins (see John 3:17), and God raised Him from the dead (see Romans 10:9; 1 Corinthians 15:14). Read and study the Bible to know who Jesus Christ is!
    - Believing and accepting Him as your personal Lord and Savior (see Romans 10:9).

2) **Confessing Jesus Christ as Lord:** The Bible says in Romans 10:9 that "if you confess with your mouth the Lord Jesus

and believe in your heart that God has raised Him from the dead, you will be saved." Confession in this verse is not a mere verbal acknowledgment of Jesus as Lord; it's a genuine personal conviction and submission of our heart to Jesus as Lord over our lives, in which we now live in the newness of life to bring glory and honor to Him. We do this by repenting of our sins and trusting in Him as our Savior who saved us from the penalty of our sins.

# CHAPTER 12

# KNOWING GOD BY HIS WORD

Once we are saved by faith in Jesus Christ, we grow in knowing God by His Word in the following ways:

1) **Through the reading, studying, and understanding of God's Word.** It is God's Word that gives us knowledge and understanding of who God is. We learn about God's mind, God's thoughts, God's nature, God's character, who God is, what God is like, God's will, and God's promises for us all from His Word.

2) **We come to know God personally not only by reading and knowing what the Bible says about God, but by our personal experience of God's Word.** For instance, as God's Word changes and transforms our lives, we come to see and know God's Word as our own lives become a witness to its infallible truth.

Let us consider just two following examples of knowing God from His Word: By His Names and By His Promises:

## KNOWING GOD BY HIS NAMES

We know someone beyond their name via our personal experience of them. In the Bible, names generally denoted who a person was (is) and their character. Similarly, it is certainly true that God's names denote who He is and His character. The study on the names of God is one of the greatest ways God has revealed Himself to man. **In knowing God by His Word and even by His Names through personal experience, we can know God's nature and character for ourselves (God's love, grace, mercy, goodness, kindness, and faithfulness) and His promises (blessings) for us.** Some of God's names denote Him as being Almighty in His Creatorship and the plurality in Him (i.e., God the Father, God the Son, God the Holy Spirit), such as "El-Shaddai" (see Genesis 17:1) and "Elohim" (see Genesis 1:1, 26; Exodus 3:1-6, 15). Other names of God reveal Him as the Redeemer in His covenant relationship with His people. In Exodus 6:2, God reveals Himself to Moses during Israel's bondage and slavery to the Egyptians. He says, "I am the LORD. I appeared to Abraham, to Isaac, and to Jacob as God Almighty [El-Shaddai], but *by* My name LORD [Jehovah or Yahweh] I was not known to them." God told Moses this to reveal how Israel would come to know and experience Him as their LORD as He redeems them (delivers them out of Egyptian bondage and slavery) and in His covenant with them.

Also, after God delivered Israel out of their Egyptian bondage and slavery through miracles, signs, and wonders, including ten plagues and the parting of the Red Sea so that they could walk through on dry ground, He led them into the wilderness to Mt. Sinai and gave them His law. There, He reminded them of who He is—LORD, their Redeemer—in Exodus 20: 2-3 (author paraphrase): "I am the LORD your God, who brought you out of Egypt, out of the place of slavery, therefore, you are not to have any other gods before me." In other words, because of who God is—their LORD, the self-sufficient One, their Redeemer and Deliverer—and what He did in covenant relationship to Israel, the correct response was to worship Him and Him alone.

One of God's names is translated as "Lord," which altogether appears well over 6,000 times in the Bible. "Lord" denotes God's eternal, sovereign, and supreme being as Redeemer, Provider, Protector, and King of His people. "Jehovah" and "Yahweh" are simply the English and Hebrew pronunciations, respectively, for God's name, translated as "LORD" (or "Lord"). This name is also closely connected to **"I AM"** as a declaration of His redemptive relationship to Israel:

> *Now therefore, behold, the cry of the children of Israel is come unto me: and I have also seen the oppression wherewith the Egyptians oppress them. Come now therefore, and I will send thee unto Pharaoh, that thou mayest bring forth my people the children of Israel out of Egypt. And Moses said unto God, Who am I, that I should go unto Pharaoh, and that I should bring forth the children of Israel out of Egypt? And he said, Certainly I will be with thee; and this shall be a token unto thee, that I have sent thee: When thou hast brought forth the people out of Egypt, ye shall serve God upon this mountain. And Moses said unto God, Behold, when I come unto the children of Israel, and shall*

*say unto them, The God of your fathers hath sent me unto you; and they shall say to me,* **What *is* his name? what shall I say unto them? And God said unto Moses, I AM THAT I AM: and he said, Thus shalt thou say unto the children of Israel, I AM hath sent me unto you."**—*Exodus 3:9-14 (KJV)*

"I AM" is a name for God that means "I am the One who is." "I AM" speaks of God's eternal being, His self-existence, and His self-sufficiency as all He ever needs to be. God's names reveal aspects of His character and who He is. Some of God's names are also compound names, such as "Jehovah-Jireh," which means "The Lord who provides" (see Genesis 22:14).

Personally, I have come to know and experience God as Provider. In Philippians 4:19, Paul the Apostle says: "And my God will supply all your need according to His riches in glory in Christ Jesus." This verse is God's promise to supply all our needs as our Provider. When I got laid off from a job (twice) as a young man just graduating from college, I really depended on and trusted in God to provide for me so that I could keep a roof over my head and pay my bills, and God did just that. I was able to find jobs, and though they were not my first choice, I happily accepted and worked them. Eventually, God opened up a door for me in a big way. I landed my first big job in engineering with nearly double the salary I asked for and gave me two big raises in the first year of my work. I knew it was all by God's grace and favor and provision, and I thanked God for it and gave Him glory!

Another name in the Bible that speaks of God's nature and character is "Jehovah Rafah" in Exodus 15:26, which means "The LORD who heals" (In the context of Exodus 15:26, God demonstrated His healing power to the people of Israel in the wilderness by purifying bitter water to make it drinkable for them to survive). God is able and still does heal physically today; for example, God can heal us through prayer (see James 5:14-16) or when we exercise faith (see Matthew 9:29), yet even when we pray or exercise faith for physical healing, God heals according to His sovereign will and choice. Ultimately, God offers to completely heal and make us whole through Jesus Christ as Isaiah 53:5 (NASB) says, "... by His wounds we are healed." Greater than physical healing is spiritual healing and wholeness_being saved and forgiven of our sins through Jesus Christ. I have personally known and experienced God as a Healer (physically and spiritually). God has healed me physically (from a cold, for instance) through orange juice, chicken soup, medicine, and Tylenol. I do my part but ultimately trust and give God the credit for my health, healing, and recovery.

The Bible also speaks to the nature and character of God as our Heavenly Father who gives us good things when we ask or pray to Him (see Matthew 7:7-11), shows us compassion (see Psalm 103:13), mercy and comfort (see 2 Corinthians 1:3-4), and even disciplines us when necessary as a loving father would a son (see Proverbs 3:11-12). Throughout my life as a Christian, I have known and experienced God as a loving Heavenly Father who has given me good things; has answered my prayers (in the best ways He sees fit); has shown me compassion, mercy, and comfort (even in the darkest moments of life); and has also corrected me when necessary, among other things, both seen and unseen.

Jesus Christ, the Son of God, is declared to be both **Savior** *and* **Lord** (see Luke 2:11; Acts 2:36). All of us are in desperate need to be saved from our sins, as the wages (or penalty) of our sins is death (see Romans 6:23).

**As Savior:** Jesus is the one and only means God has provided to forgive and save us from the penalty of our sins (see Matthew 1:21; Acts 2:42-43, 4:12; 1 Timothy 1:15; 1 John 2:2), from the power of sin (see Romans 6:6) and from the works and power of the devil/Satan (see 1 John 3:8). Jesus Christ is also our Savior, our help, our hope in time of need or anything we might going through today (see Hebrews 4:15-16; 1 Peter 5:7).

**As Lord:** Jesus is God (see John 20:28). He is alive and risen from the dead (see Romans 10:9) and has all authority in heaven and on earth (see Matthew 28:18). When we confess and place our faith in Jesus Christ as our Lord and Savior (see Romans 10:9-10), we are forgiven and saved from the penalty and power of sin and are given eternal life with God. Now, we must follow, obey, and honor Jesus as our personal Lord and Savior.

Table 5 is a non-exhaustive list of God's names found in the Bible. All His names are also traits and aspects of His Son Jesus Christ.

| TABLE 5: **NAMES OF GOD THAT DENOTES HIS CHARACTER** | | |
|---|---|---|
| GOD'S NAME | MEANING | REFERENCES |
| El-Shaddai | The Almighty God | Exodus 6:3 |

| | | |
|---|---|---|
| El-Elyon | The Most High God or Exalted One | Numbers 24:16; 2 Samuel 22:14; Psalms 18:13 |
| El-Olam | God of Eternity or the Everlasting God | Genesis 21:33; Isaiah 26:4; Psalms 90:2 |
| El-Roi | The God who Sees Me | Genesis 16:13 |
| Elohim | Describes the plurality in God (God the Father, God the Son, God the Holy Spirit) | Genesis 1:1, 26 |
| Lord (Jehovah or Yahweh; YHWH in Hebrew) | God's covenant name that is most frequently used in the Scriptures. It affirms God's eternal and sovereign being, authority, power, and lordship over all creation and as redeemer, provider, protector, and king of His people. | Exodus 6:2, 20:1 |
| I AM | Denotes God's self-existence and self-sufficiency | Exodus 3:14 |
| Jehovah-Jireh | The Lord who Provides | Genesis 22:14 |
| Jehovah-Mekaddesh | The Lord who Sanctifies | Exodus 31:13 |
| Jehovah-Shalom | The Lord of Peace. When we make our peace with God through Jesus Christ and are forgiven of our sins, we can truly live and walk in the peace of God | Judges 6:24 |

| Jehovah-Saboath | The Lord of Hosts | 1 Samuel 1:3; 17:45 |
|---|---|---|
| Jehovah-Rohi | The Lord is my Shepherd | Psalms 23:1 |
| Heavenly Father | God Our Heavenly Father | John 1:12; 1 Corinthians 8:6; 1 John 3:1 |
| Jesus Christ [Also called the Word of God (John 1:1)] | The Son of God (God Incarnate); Savior and Lord | Luke 2:11; Acts 2:36 |
| A name no one knows but Him | Even though there are names of God in the Bible that describe His traits and attributes, we will never be able to fully understand God's eternal and infinite being and His greatness. Therefore, He has a name that no one knows but Him. | Revelation 19:12 |

## KNOWING GOD BY HIS PROMISES

It is awesome to know God when you experience His promises in your life! One of my favorite promises in the Bible that I have seen God do repeatedly in my life is Romans 8:28 (author paraphrase): "We know that all things work together for good to them who love God and are the called according to His purpose." Notice how the Apostle Paul says "**We** know," referring to everyone who has a relationship with God through Jesus Christ. "We" are those who love God and are the called according to His purpose.

Table 6 delineates a few of God's promises for His people.

| TABLE 6: **GOD'S PROMISES TO HIS PEOPLE** ||
|---|---|
| PROMISES | SCRIPTURE |
| • God has promised every spiritual blessing to His people through Jesus Christ.<br>• We are chosen by God before the foundation (creation) of the world.<br>• We are predestined by God to be adopted as His son (or daughter) through Jesus Christ.<br>• We have redemption and forgiveness of sins, according to the riches of God's grace.<br>• We are sealed (protected) by the Holy Spirit until the day of redemption (heaven). God's Holy Spirit comes to indwell and secure and preserve a person they place their faith in Jesus Christ as Savior and Lord (Ephesians 1:13-14; Romans 10:9-10). | Ephesians 1:3-14 |
| • For those who love God and are called according to His purpose, He promises to work all things together for their good. | Romans 8:28 |
| • God promises to never leave nor forsake His people. | Matthew 28:20; John 14:16-19 |
| • God promises to be a very present Help to His people in the time of trouble. | Psalm 46:1 |
| • For those who keep God's commandments, He promises the fullness of joy. | John 15:9-11 |

## LIVING IN THE SAFETY OF **GOD'S SECRET PLACE**

| | |
|---|---|
| • For those who pray to God and put their trust in Him, He promises a peace that surpasses all understanding. | Isaiah 26:3; Philippians 4:6-7 |
| • God promises to answer the prayers of those who ask and pray according to God's will. | 1 John 5:19 |
| • God promises to give good things to those who ask. | Matthew 7:11 |
| • God promises to provide and take care of the needs of those who love Him. | Luke 12: 22-28 |
| • God promises His very presence by His Holy Spirit and help and comfort to those who love and follow Him. | John 14: 16-19 |
| • God promises comfort to His people in their trials and troubles. | 2 Corinthians 1:3-4 |
| • God promises grace and strength to His people in their weakness. | 2 Corinthians 12:9 |
| • God promises His protection to those who abide in His presence. | Psalms 91 |
| • God promises to lead and guide those who seek and put their trust in Him. | Proverbs 3:5-6; James 1:5 |
| • God promises to reward those who diligently seek after Him in faith. | Hebrews 11:6 |
| • God promises His people the moment they die, their soul/spirit will be in His presence. | 2 Corinthians 5:6-8 |

| | |
|---|---|
| • God promises His people a bodily resurrection from the dead with new glorified spiritual bodies like the resurrected Christ. | 1 Corinthians 15:35-58 |
| • God promises His people that as they suffer for Christ, they will be glorified and reign with Christ. | 2 Timothy 2:12 |

*I encourage you to read and study the Bible for yourself so that you may learn about God's nature, character, and promises, and know God personally and experience Him for yourself!*

# CHAPTER 13

# KNOWING GOD THROUGH SUFFERING

Oh, we may not like this one!!! If we're completely honest, none of us would ever choose to hurt or suffer, but hurting and suffering always gives us the opportunity to know God, His goodness, His faithfulness, His power, His love, His mercy, and His grace in ways that we may not have learned in comfort. When we suffer, we come to know God as He shows up in His grace to carry us through. In 2 Corinthians 12:9, the Apostle Paul prayed and pleaded with God to remove something unpleasant from his life. Have you ever had moments like that, where you asked: "Why am I going through this? Why me?" I know I have certainly had moments like that in my life!

The Book of Ephesians talks about the riches of God's grace, and God also gives us sufficient grace to deal with every situation as it pertains to this life. God even gives us grace to deal with and take us through our suffering, including our grief and loss. The Apostle Paul knew why he was suffering; he was given a thorn in the flesh, lest he would be exalted beyond measure, and Paul again prayed and pleaded with God to remove it. God didn't remove it, but instead, He gave Paul sufficient grace to deal with it and take him through it. As much as we may like to avoid suffering, God may not always necessarily save us from it, but in any case, God will give us the sufficient grace that we need to endure it. His grace is sufficient for you. He didn't say that His grace *was* sufficient or His grace *will be* sufficient. No! **His grace is sufficient for you and His strength is made perfect in your weakness.**

When we claim to be strong in ourselves, in our own strength, in our own abilities, in our own wisdom and knowledge, we can't see God, but in our weakness, in our place of brokenness, we are more readily available to see the power and grace of God demonstrated in our lives. That is something I have also learned through God's comfort. I remember the pain, heartbreak, grief, loss, disappointments, setbacks, and all hell breaking loose, but I just shake my head because I know that if it was not for God, I wouldn't have made it. I would've lost my mind, but God kept me, preserved me, and carried me through those things because His grace was sufficient for me, and His grace is sufficient for you also.

# CHAPTER 14

# KNOWING GOD BY HIS HOLY SPIRIT

The Holy Spirit is not some impersonal force! The Holy Spirit is the very person, presence and power of God. When we enter into a personal relationship with God through faith in Jesus Christ and accept Him as our personal Savior and Lord, God's Holy Spirit immediately comes to indwell and live inside of us (Romans 8:9; Ephesians 4:30). As a result, we can get to know God through His Holy Spirit who now lives and resides inside of us. The Apostle Paul gives a declaration to the church at Corinth in his day in 2 Corinthians 13:14. He says: "The grace of the Lord Jesus Christ, and the love of God, and the fellowship [communion] of the Holy Spirit, be with you all" (NIV). In the Bible, "fellowship" or "communion" comes from a Greek word that means to share and have personal, intimate fellowship and partnership with someone. We can have a personal, intimate fellowship, sharing, and partnership with the Holy Spirit in the following ways (not an exhaustive list):

1) **Through Prayer:** We fellowship with God through the Holy Spirit by praying and talking to Him (see Chapter 18: Practical Application #1: A Strong Prayer Life). God also talks and fellowship with us through His Holy Spirit (see Chapter 15 under #2 Holy Spirit). The fellowship with God through prayer helps us to grow in our fellowship and relationship with God and our knowing of Him.

2) **Through Revelation and Illumination:** We get to know God through His Holy Spirit because it is the Holy Spirit that reveals to us the things of God. Note the two following passages the Apostle Paul shares in his letter to the Christians in the church at Corinth in reference to Holy Spirit's relationship with them:

- 1 Corinthians 2:10-11 (ESV): "For the Spirit searches everything, even the depths of God. For who knows a person's thoughts except the spirit of that person, which is in him? So also no one comprehends the thoughts of God except the Spirit of God."

- 1 Corinthians 2:12-14 (NASB): Now we have not received the spirit of the world, but the Spirit who is from God, so that we may know the things freely given to us by God. We also speak these things, not in words taught by human wisdom, but in those taught by the Spirit, combining spiritual *thoughts* with spiritual *words*. But a natural person does not accept the things of the Spirit of God, for they are foolishness to him; and he cannot understand them, because they are spiritually discerned.

In other words, the Apostle Paul is saying it is God's Holy Spirit that He gives to us, so that we may be able to receive and understand the things of God. Apart from the Holy Spirit, we are not able to receive or understand the things of God; the Holy Spirit is what gives us both revelation and illumination of God and His truth (see also John 16:13). Therefore, we get to know God and grow in our fellowship and relationship with Him by means of the Holy Spirit's revelation to us and His illumination of our knowledge and understanding of God.

3) **Through Transformation:** When we surrender to the leading of the Holy Spirit, we surrender to God and what He desires to do both in and through our lives. In this, God transforms us and our lives for His glory and honor. More specifically, as we surrender to the Holy Spirit's work in our lives, God transforms our character to be like Him. The Apostle Paul writes to the church in Galatia about the fruit of the Spirit which are traits of God's character in the following verse:

- Galatians 5:22-23 (ESV): "But the fruit of the Spirit is love, joy, peace, patience, kindness, goodness, faithfulness, gentleness, self-control; against such things there is no law."

The more time you spend with anyone, quite naturally some of them rub off on you, and you begin to sound and even act like that person. I have spent about four years with the beautiful lady Isabel, who is now my wife. We sound and act like each other because of the time we have spent together. Similarly, when we spend time with God in our fellowship and relationship with Him, He actually transforms us to be more and more like Him, and we begin to exemplify the character traits (fruit) of His Holy Spirit at work in our lives: love, joy, peace, patience, kindness, goodness, faithfulness, gentleness, and self-control.

However, as I previously mentioned, God's Holy Spirit is a gentleman. He will never force or impose Himself on us. Our fellowship with the Holy Spirit is a willing partnership in which we surrender to God and allow Him to be the Lord of our lives.

# CHAPTER 15

# KNOWING GOD BY HIS VOICE

We need to know and recognize God's voice to know Him personally. Some common questions come up for us when it comes to hearing from God. "How do you hear God's voice?" "How do you know when God is speaking?" "When does God speak?" "How does God speak?" "Will God speak to me?"

Growing up, I admired how my mother was such a praying woman with a very close personal relationship with God and was also sensitive to God's voice. I would often hear my mother say: "God is speaking," "God is saying this," or "God is saying that." It always fascinated me because I too wanted to hear God's voice; I wanted God to speak to me! Yet as I got older, I recognized that my mother wasn't audibly hearing from God. That was a major revelation for me because it helped me understand how to recognize how God speaks to me personally! **We should think of God's voice as His means of communing and communicating**

**with us in our fellowship and relationship with Him** (see John 10:27-29, 16:13; Revelation 3:20). Because God desires to make Himself known to us (see John 5:39, 17:3) and have fellowship and a relationship with us (see James 4:8), He wants to commune and communicate with us (see 1 John 1:3).

Numerous illustrations in the Bible depict our personal relationship with God. One is found in John 10, where God's people (those who are saved and have a personal relationship with Him) are illustrated as Jesus' sheep, and Jesus Himself is referred to as the Good Shepherd who lays down His life for His sheep (see John 10:11). In John 10:1-5, Jesus declares that His sheep hear His voice and that He calls His own sheep by name; He calls them out and His sheep follows Him, for they know His voice. They won't follow a stranger's voice. In fact, they will flee from it, for they know not the voice of strangers.

A few facts about sheep:
- They cannot see very well or very far.
- They can easily wander off.
- They can't defend themselves or run very fast when a predator, like a wolf, pursues them.

Sheep need provision, protection, and guidance, and shepherds were especially common back in biblical times. You'll also find throughout the Bible where God (Jesus) relates to His people as the Shepherd and refers to His people as His sheep (see Psalms 23:1; John 10:1-5). Therefore, God's people—His sheep—have the privilege of enjoying His provision, His protection, and His guidance in their lives. Even King David, who was a shepherd himself, wrote in Psalm 23:1, "The LORD *is* my shepherd; I shall not want." David understood what a shepherd did, so he knew that God was his—his Provider, Protector, and Guide. **God's sheep are His people who have fellowship and a relationship with Him through Jesus Christ; therefore, those who are God's sheep will hear and know His voice (see John 10:3-4).**

The reason why sheep hear and know their shepherd's voice is because they have spent time with their shepherd (see John 10:1-5). Therefore, learning how to hear and know God's voice involves spending time with Him. Two of the most practical ways to spend time with God are to read, study, and meditate on His written Word and talk to God in prayer When you think about it, you would recognize and know a good friend's voice only if you had spent adequate time with that person and have a relationship with them. For example, if a stranger calls you on the phone, chances are you will not recognize their voice. Why? Because you don't know the person; you don't have any previous affiliation or relationship with that person; you haven't spent time with that person. But if a good friend calls you on the phone, you will recognize his or her voice because you have a relationship with that person. **Similarly, to recognize God's voice, you must tend to your relationship and spend time with Him so that when He does speak to you, you will know it's Him (and when it is not!).**

When you think about the closet personal relationships that you have, most of them, if not all, have probably come about as a result of spending the time, effort, and commitment to grow in those relationships; you won't grow in any meaningful relationship without investing time and effort into it. We also must invest time and effort to grow in our relationship with God. **The more time we spend with God, the more we will recognize and know God's voice when He speaks, and the more our relationship**

**with Him will grow.** Jesus says in John 10:14-15: "I am the good Shepherd, and I know my sheep, and am known by My own." As Jesus illustrates in this verse, sheep will recognize and know their shepherd and his voice when they spend time with the shepherd. The word "know" in John 10:14-15 means more than just: "I know your name" or "I know something about you." It means to know someone personally. **God's (Jesus') sheep are His people whom He knows personally, and He is also personally known by them.**

So how does God speak to us?

### 1) By His written Word (the Bible)

The primary way that God speaks to us is through His written Word. Second Timothy 3:16 says: "All scripture *is* given by inspiration of God and is profitable for doctrine [teaching], for reproof, for correction, for instruction in righteousness." The Bible provides everything you need to know about God's nature, God's character, God's thoughts, and to live out God's will, purpose, and plan for your life. **Therefore, reading and studying God's Word is one of the most practical ways to spend time with God and learn to recognize His voice as we grow in our knowledge, fellowship, and relationship with Him.** We also grow in our knowledge of God through personal experience as we live by the Bible and make it practical in our lives.

Because God created us, loves us, and knows what is best for us (in His infinite wisdom and knowledge of us as our Creator), He desires for us to know His will, purpose, and plans for our lives. **Nothing is more rewarding, satisfying, or fulfilling than knowing and walking in God's will for your life.** Satan knows that and doesn't want us to spend time reading the Bible; it's why he tries to distract or discourage us from reading the Bible. He likes it when we're too busy or too tired to read the Bible. He loves to see our Bibles collect dust. **If we're serious about knowing God's voice and growing in our relationship with Him, we have to make reading, studying, and meditating on the Word of God daily part of our lifestyle.**

We are often discouraged from reading the Bible because it seems too hard to read or understand. But the Bible says that God "is a rewarder of those that diligently seek him" (Hebrews 11:6, KJV). He will find and reward those who genuinely and diligently seek Him. We can't understand the Scriptures on our own anyway; it is the illumination of the Holy Spirit that allows us to understand the Holy Scriptures of the Bible. It is the Holy Spirit who leads and guides us into all truth—the truth of the Scriptures in the Word of God.

God speaks to us in many ways.

## 2) The Holy Spirit

God speaks to us through His Holy Spirit. The Holy Spirit brings God's Word to our remembrance (see John 14:26), sharing what He hears from God with us (see John 16:13). He may share things that are to come (see John 16:13); He may teach and guide us into God's truth (see John 14:26, 16:12-14; 1 Corinthians 2:11-16); He may transform and renew our mind (or impress something upon our heart and mind) with God's thoughts or desires (see Psalms 37:4; Romans 12:2; 1 Corinthians 12:16; Philippians 2:13); or He may lead (prompt) us to act on something according to God's Word or God's will (see Romans

8:14; Galatians 5:16-25; Philippians 2:13; Acts 8:29, 10:19, 11:12, 13:2, 16:7-8).

In John 14:25-26, after Jesus' ascension, the Holy Spirit brought to their remembrance the things Jesus had said to them so that they could write the New Testament Scriptures. **The application for us today is that when we read, study, and meditate on the Word of God, the Holy Spirit will also bring God's Word to our remembrance.** On numerous occasions, the Holy Spirit has brought to my remembrance something that I read from God's Word when I needed it at that particular time in my life.

I remember a time in college when I was working at McDonald's part-time. After my last day of work, I came to pick up my final paycheck. I had my whole uniform with me to return but didn't have my name tag. One of the young managers there gave me a hard time; he rudely yelled at me in a lobby full of customers: "WELL, I CAN'T GIVE YOU YOUR CHECK BECAUSE YOU DON'T HAVE YOUR NAME TAG!!" Then, he shoved my uniform back at me over the counter. I was so upset that I had thoughts of jacking the manager up over the counter and demanding that he give me my check. Yet, the Holy Spirit convicted me that following through with those thoughts wouldn't be the right course of action. He brought Scriptures to my remembrance such as Proverbs 14:29 (NASB), which says: "One who is slow to anger has great understanding; But one who is quick-tempered exalts foolishness." As the Holy Spirit brought Scriptures to my remembrance, it convicted me against doing the wrong thing (such as being quick-tempered and jacking the manger up over the counter) and led me to act on God's Word instead (be slow to anger, don't lose your temper, just walk away and come back later). So that's what I did and when I came back, another manager had seen how the younger manager acted towards me and gave me my final check without asking any questions. In a heated moment, I thanked God that I surrendered to the Holy Spirit's voice and was lead to do the right thing.

**One of the Holy Spirit's most valuable ministries is bringing God's Word to our remembrance as we need it.** But if we don't read, study, and meditate on God's Word, then the Holy Spirit won't have much to bring to our remembrance. That's why it is all the more important to make reading the Bible a daily priority in our life, to be enriched with the Word of God, so the Holy Spirit can bring it to our remembrance as we need it. God will use other people and other means (i.e., dreams, circumstances, etc.) to bring scripture to remembrance.

**How can we know whether Holy Spirit is speaking (or not speaking)?** Well, Jesus says in John 16:13 that the Holy Spirit would not speak by His own authority but by whatever He heard His Father speak. Therefore, the Holy Spirit will only remind, affirm, or speak God's Word to us and lead us to act and do according to God's will. In other words, if we sense or feel that the Holy Spirit is speaking to us or leading us to do something that is inconsistent with God's will (see Philippians 2:13) and/or God's nature and character (see Galatians 5:22-23), then it is not the Holy Spirit. The Holy Spirit will never speak or lead us to do something that goes against God's will, nature, and character!

Though the Holy Spirit (God) can speak to us audibly (as in God speaking in a literal voice from heaven), it's not typical; most of us will never hear the Holy Spirit (God) speak to us audibly. Typically, the Holy Spirit will speak to us by reminding us of God's Word, affirming God's Word to us, convicting us of God's Word, and/or impressing God's Word, will, thoughts, and desires upon our hearts or minds (see John 14:26, 16:12-14; 1 Corinthians 2:11-16; Psalm 37:4; Philippians 2:13). Also, when you are led by the Holy Spirit, He will never force you to do something; the Holy Spirit will instead gently prompt or urge you to do and/or act according to God's Word and will. You must surrender to prompting if you want Him to lead you (see Romans 8:14; Galatians 5:16-25). In Acts 8:29, the Holy Spirit told Phillip the missionary to go near to the chariot of the Ethiopian to help him understand the scriptures he was reading and to share the gospel with him. In the case of Phillip in Acts Chapter 8, it's possible that he could have heard the Holy Spirit speak audibly or the Holy Spirit could have simply convicted him or impressed upon his heart and mind to go near to the chariot of the Ethiopian to share the gospel with him. In Acts 10:19 and 11:12, the Holy Spirit spoke to Peter in a vision to go with certain men We aren't sure whether God spoke to Peter audibly or through a prompting or impression. Personally, I have never heard the Holy Spirit speak to me audibly (and honestly, if He ever did, it would probably freak me out), but the Holy Spirit has and does speak to me—He reminds me of God's Word, affirms God's Word to me, convicts me of God's Word, and impresses God's Word, will, thoughts and desires upon my heart and mind.

The Holy Spirit may also speak to us and/or lead us circumstantially or providentially. In Acts 16:7-8, the Holy Spirit forbade Paul, Silas, and Timothy to preach in Asia and stopped them from going into Bithynia. This passage doesn't explicitly tell us how the Holy Spirit forbade or stopped them. He could have stopped them through circumstances or providentially.

## 3) Our Conscience

Our conscience is our inner, intuitive sense of right and wrong (see Romans 1:19; 2:12); it allows us to contemplate our motives and actions and evaluate and judge what we believe to be right and wrong (see Romans 2:14-15). Our conscience works best when it is trained and informed by the Word of God (see Psalms 119:11). Many times, Apostle Paul warned Christian believers not to violate their conscience or others (see Romans 13:5; 1 Corinthians 8:7, 12; 10:25, 29; 2 Corinthians 5:11; Acts 23:1) or repeatedly ignore the warnings of our conscience for risk of desensitizing or even silencing it (see 1 Timothy 4:2). Finally, Paul encourages Timothy, his spiritual son, to love from a pure heart and a good conscience (see 1Timothy 1:5), because our intuitive sense of right and wrong makes the conscience self-judging (see Romans 2:15). In other words, when we violate what we sense or believe to be right, our conscience produces guilt (see 1 John 3:21). On the other hand, when we do what we sense or believe to be right, especially based on God's Word, we will have the affirmation, assurance, peace, and joy of a good and clear conscience (1 Timothy 1:5).

## 4) Dreams

A dream can be defined as a projection of images in the mind that a person sees when they are asleep, producing emotions and physical sensations. God sometimes speaks or reveals things to us dreams (see Genesis 37:1-11, 40:1-23, 41:1-32;

Deuteronomy 13:1-5; Daniel 2:1-45; Mathew 1:20-21, 2:13, 19-20). For instance, in Mathew 1:20-21, 2:13, and 19-20, God spoke to Joseph, Mary's husband, through dreams. He gave him very specific instructions about keeping the child Jesus and Mary safe from King Herod. Even though God can speak to us through dreams, we shouldn't limit or expect God to only speak to us that way. Dreams seem to be an exception, not the primary way God speaks. Even though dreams can be of God (see previous scripture references), sometimes dreams are meaningless (see Ecclesiastes 5:7) or occur because of our worries and concerns (see Ecclesiastes 5:3).

God would often reveal things to my mother in a dream. So, when I was younger, I made the mistake of thinking that if God spoke to me, it would be through a dream, but I never was and still am not much of a dreamer. Now I won't say that God has never spoken or shown me something through a dream, but I can probably count on a single hand how many dreams God has used to speak to me or show me something. Most of the time, my dreams are random and meaningless (see Ecclesiastes 5:7). Therefore, dreams are not the primary way I expect God to speak to me. Instead, He tends to speak to me primarily through His Word and the Holy Spirit. Some people regularly dream. They are "dreamers" (see Deuteronomy 13:1), but not everybody is not a dreamer.

In any case, God gives us His criteria for evaluating dreams (see Deuteronomy 13:1-5). Typically, if or when God does speak or reveal something through a dream, He will confirm the dream and/or bring it to pass (see Genesis 40:1-23, 41:1-57; Daniel 2:1-45). Of course, if you're really not sure if a dream is of God, it's good to pray and talk to God about it. Ask Him if there's something He wants to say or show you. It may also be useful to talk to someone (a trusted source you know) who may have the God-given gift of dream interpretation. One way or another, if God uses a dream to speak or reveal something to you, He'll also give understanding and confirm it in your reality (see Matthew 1:20-21, 2:13, 19-20).

**5) Visions**

God can sometimes speak or communicate through visions (see Isaiah 6:1-7; Jeremiah 1:11-19; Ezekiel 1:4-28; Daniel 7:1-28; 8:1-27; Amos 7:1-9, 8:1, 9:1; Zachariah 1:7; 6:8; Acts 10:9-15). Visions might be described as seeing a dream with your eyes open. In Acts 10:9-15, God spoke to Peter and showed him something through a vision after he had gone to the rooftop to pray and fell into a trance. But similar to dreams, don't limit God by expecting a vision to be the only way or even God's primary way of speaking to you.

**6) Audible Voice**

As we see in the Bible, God may speak to us audibly (see Genesis 12:1; Matthew 3:17; Acts 9:7). We should, however, understand that God has already spoken and will speak to us by what He has already revealed to us through His written Word and by the Holy Spirit (who normally doesn't speak in an audible voice); therefore, God rarely speaks in an audible voice. Yet, if God desires or even sees the need to speak to us audibly, He will certainly do it.

## 7) Circumstances

God can speak to us circumstantially. For instance, God used circumstances to lead Joseph and Mary to Bethlehem, because of the prophecy that Jesus was to be born in Bethlehem. Mary was on the verge of giving birth to Jesus when they were in a town called Nazareth, but it was also a time when the Roman emperor Caesar Augustus decreed that everyone go to Bethlehem and register for the census. God used those circumstances to lead Joseph and Mary to Bethlehem, so Jesus would be born there according to the prophecy (see Micah 5:2). Even in my own life, God has spoken to or led me by circumstances. For instance, I've applied for jobs that I thought would be a good fit, God knew better than I did and kept those doors shut. All along, God was leading me to a job or opportunity that was better and in line with His will and purpose for me.

## 8) Heavenly Messengers

God can speak to us through heavenly messengers (i.e., angels) (Genesis 18:1-15; 32:24-32; Judges 6:11-23, 13:1-21; Daniel 7:16; 8:13-16; 9:22-27; Matthew 1:20-25; 2:13, 19-20; Luke 1:11-20, 26-38, 2:9-15). Hebrews 13:2 (KJV) says: "Be not forgetful to entertain [or show hospitality to] strangers: for thereby some have entertained [or have shown hospitality] to angels unaware." That Scripture encourages us to show hospitality even to strangers because they could be angels sent by God to bless or communicate a promise or message. Samson's father is a great example. At first, he wasn't aware that the man was an angel of God sent to him and his wife to prophesize their child's (Samson) birth and purpose to deliver the Israelites from oppression (see Judges 13:3-21).

## 9) People

God can speak to us through other people (see Exodus 7:6-7; 2 Samuel 12:1-15; 1 Kings 11:31, 12:24). Particularly in the Old Testament, He often spoke to the people of Israel as a group through His leaders and prophets (see Exodus 3:1-15, 33:1-23; Isaiah 6:8-13; Jeremiah 2:1-37; Ezekiel 2:1-6) and also through the people who made up the local church body (particularly in the New Testament). God speaks to the people of the church as a group through the pastor or messenger (i.e., preacher, teacher, prophet) of the church (see Romans 10:14-15; Ephesians 4:11; 1 Timothy 5:17; Revelation 2:1-3:22). While God does speak to the people of the church through the pastor or messenger, it is very important to recognize the voice of God so that you know whether God is speaking to you through him or her. While the pastor(s) are to serve, lead, and guide the local church body (as they are led by God) and teach God's Word, it's important to evaluate the message by weighing it against God's Word. For example, in Acts 17:11, the Berean Jews studied and searched the scriptures to verify the teachings of the Apostle Paul and Silas against the Word of God and through discernment of the Holy Spirit (see 1 John 4; 1 Thessalonians 5:21). It is important for the Church to know the voice of God and God's Word because there are many false teachers and prophets (see Matthew 7:15; 2 Corinthians 11:13-15; 1 John 4:1; 2 Peter 2:1-3), and you can be deceived or lead astray if you don't recognize the voice of God (see Ephesians 4:14). A pastor or messenger is appointed to lead the church into the truth of God's Word, but they are also human and capable of error. Even the Apostle Paul recognized this in prophets in the church and encouraged the people of the church not to despise prophecies (or teachings from church leaders, for that matter), but to test all things and hold fast to that which is good (see 1 Thessalonians 5:21). We must weigh all teachings against what God says in His written Word and learn to discern through the Holy Spirit to test (assess and evaluate) its legitimacy (see Acts 17:11; 1 John 4:1).

As a minister of God's Word, I'm particularly hard on Bible teachers and preachers because I understand the difference between good and bad Hermeneutics (the method of Bible interpretation) when I hear a message, but beyond that, as a seasoned Christian, I can immediately recognize when God is using a person to speak and when God is not because of my knowledge, continuing study of God's Word, and growing spiritual discernment. I have seen pastors and leaders share with the church (and even with me personally) a word they felt God had given them. I have found that, in many cases, I have known without a doubt that they are messengers of God. On the other hand, I have also picked up on and sensed when messengers are self-proclaimed and not sent by God.

All that to say—God can and does use people to speak to His congregation in the church setting through pastors and other messengers (see 1 Corinthians 14:25). He also uses common, everyday people to speak directly to us (see Hebrews 13:2). In either case, it's important for us to recognize and know God's voice and God's Word for ourselves and to test the message that we hear. Anything that is good or of God is what we should hold onto and anything that is not good or of God is what we should reject (eat the meat but throw the bones away). The Apostle Paul says it this way in 1 Thessalonians 5:21 (author paraphrase: **"test all things and hold fast to that which is good."**

You may not always hear, "I feel God wants me to tell you something." Sometimes God will speak through someone in an ordinary or random conversation that will gently nudge your spirit to listen. Also, God can speak through the wise and godly counsel of people (see Exodus 18:1-27; Psalms 1:1; Proverbs 11:14, 15:22, 24:6).

## SUMMARY OF OUR RELATIONSHIP WITH THE TRIUNE GOD

Tables 7-9 list practical applications for nurturing our relationship with all three persons of the Trinity.

### TABLE 7: GOD'S RELATIONSHIP WITH US

**Becoming God's child by spiritual rebirth (regeneration):** When you place your faith in Jesus Christ the Son of God, you are spiritually born again into God's kingdom and become a child of God (John 1:12, 3:1-19; Romans 8:16; Galatians 3:26; 1 John 3:1). With God as your loving heavenly Father, you can pray and depend on Him as His child for His full provisional care, including His guidance (Psalms 119:105; James 1:5; 2 Timothy 3:16-17), provision for your needs (Matthew 6:25-33, 7:8-11), and protection (Matthew 6:9-13). God furthermore shows you compassion (Psalms 103:13) and even corrects or disciplines you when necessary, as a loving father would a child (Proverbs 3:11-12). *(cont'd. on next page)*

Furthermore, when you place your faith in Jesus Christ the Son of God, you are adopted into God's family as His son (or daughter) (Romans 8:15; Ephesians 1:5). As a son (or daughter) of God, you are also an heir of God and joint heir with Christ (Romans 8:17)—everything that is God's is also yours. You can enjoy all of the same rights, blessings, benefits, and privileges as Jesus Christ the Son of God (Romans 8:15-17).

## GOD AS OUR HEAVENLY FATHER

**His Guidance:** Remember that God as our Heavenly Father and Creator is all-knowing (Reference attributes of God in Chapter 3), which means He knows everything about us and knows us better than we know ourselves. (Luke 12:7 says He knows the very number of hairs on your head!) Therefore, we can trust that our Heavenly Father knows what is good and best for us, and because of His love for us, He desires to guide us so we can have, live, and enjoy the very best life that He intended through His Son Jesus Christ (John 10:10) to accomplish His will, purpose, and plan for our lives. Ultimately only God and His will can bring us true joy, peace, satisfaction, and fulfillment in life (Psalms 37:4; Proverbs 19:23).

**His Provision (Supplying Our Needs):** God as our loving Heavenly Father desires to meet and supply our needs. Because of God's love for us, He desires us not to worry about our needs (or anything for that matter), but to pray, trust, and depend on Him to meet and supply all of our needs (Psalms 23:1; Matthew 6:25-33, 7:8-11; Philippians 4: 8-9, 19).

**His Protection:** God as our loving Heavenly Father desires to protect us, yet God's protection does not necessarily exempt us from hardships, troubles, calamity, or evil. God's protection may involve protecting, keeping, and sustaining us through these things by His grace (2 Corinthians 12:9). God's protection is found in the promises of His grace to work all things together for the good of those who love Him and are called according to His purpose (Romans 8:28). Though God intends to protect us, we should not test (or tempt) God (i.e., don't deliberately put ourselves in harm's way! Don't walk in front of a bus or jump off a bridge to see if God will protect you!). Walking in obedience to God's Word and by His wisdom will protect us! In other words, protection from spiritual and even physical harm is optimized when we are walking in obedience to God's Word and by His wisdom. Ultimately, when we enter into a relationship with God the Father through Jesus Christ, the Holy Spirit comes to permanently indwell and seal us until the day of redemption in which we will have God's permanent protection from Satan and the penalty of our sins (hell) and death. Instead, we will have eternal life with God the Father. We will never lose our salvation.

### TABLE 8: **OUR PERSONAL RELATIONSHIP WITH CHRIST (GOD THE SON)**

#### CHRIST AS OUR SAVIOR

Christ is our Savior because He saves us from the guilt, punishment, and the power of our sins when we confess and repent of our sins, believe that God Has raised Him from the dead after He died on the cross for our sins, and accept and confess Him as our personal Lord and Savior (Romans 10:9-10).

#### CHRIST AS OUR LORD

Christ is Lord whether we have a personal relationship with Him or not, because God the Father has given Him all power and authority in heaven and earth (Matthew 28:18; Acts 2:36). Furthermore, every knee shall bow, and every tongue shall confess that He is Lord to the glory of God the Father (Philippians 2:9-11). When we enter into a personal relationship with Christ, He not only becomes our personal Savior; He also

| |
|---|
| becomes our personal Lord (Master) as we surrender our lives to Him, love Him, worship Him, and live according to His will, purpose, and plan for our lives to bring glory and honor to Him. |
| **CHRIST AS OUR SHEPHERD** |
| When we enter into a personal relationship with Christ, we will come to know Him (God) personally and experientially as a Shepherd, through our communion and fellowship with Him that is cultivated in prayer, reading and studying the Word, meditation, applying (obeying) His Word, and by the Holy Spirit, in which we will abide under the care of His guidance, provision, and protection as His sheep (Psalms 23; John 10). |

| |
|---|
| **TABLE 9: OUR PERSONAL RELATIONSHIP WITH GOD THE HOLY SPIRIT** |
| **THE HOLY SPIRIT'S RELATIONSHIP WITH US** |
| When you enter a personal relationship with God through Jesus Christ, His Holy Spirit comes to indwell and live inside of you (Romans 8:9; Ephesians 4:30), and then you come to know God (Christ) personally and experientially by His power (the Holy Spirit) at work in your life. It is the Holy Spirit's power that changes and transforms our lives for the glory of God (2 Corinthians 3:18), empowers us for God's service (Acts 1:8), and enables us to live the Christian life (Galatians 5:22-25; Philippians 2:13). |
| **THE HOLY SPIRIT AS OUR COMFORTER (HELPER)** |
| **His Sealing**: The Holy Spirit seals us unto the day of redemption (Ephesians 1:13, 4:30).<br>**His Empowerment**: The Holy Spirit empowers us for God's use |

and service (Acts 1:8; 1 Corinthians 12:1-11; Philippians 2:13) to live the Christian life and exemplify God's nature and character (Galatians 5:22-23).
**His Illumination**: The Holy Spirit illuminates our understanding of God's Word and truth (1 Corinthians 2:12).
**His Guidance**: The Holy Spirit leads and guides us into God's truth (John 16:13) and into God's will (Philippians 2:13).
**His Transformation**: The Holy Spirit changes and transforms our lives for the glory of God (2 Corinthians 3:18).
**His Intercession**: When we don't know what to pray for as we ought, the Holy Spirit will intercede for us (Romans 8:26).

**There is a big difference between knowing something(s) about somebody and knowing them personally.** One of my favorite basketball players of all time is Michael Jordan; I know a lot of his basketball stats, how long he played in the NBA, I know where he was born (Brooklyn NY), who his parents are (James R. Jordan Sr and Deloris Jordan), what school he went to (UNC), etc.; I have all of this information about Michael Jordan, but I don't know Michael Jordan personally nor does He know me personally.

To know God is to know Him personally and experientially through a redemptive relationship through His Son Jesus Christ. We come to know the Triune God (God the Father, Jesus Christ the Son, the Holy Spirit) through our personal fellowship, relationship, and experience with Him.

Communion comes from a Greek word that means to have a personal, intimate fellowship, sharing, and partnership with someone. You can have intimate communion with the Triune God—God the Father (see 1 John 1:3); God the Son, Jesus Christ (see 1 Corinthians 1:9; 1 John 1:3); and God the Holy Spirit (see 2 Corinthians 13:14). Your relationship with all three will determine the degree in which you will hear God's voice.

# PART 4

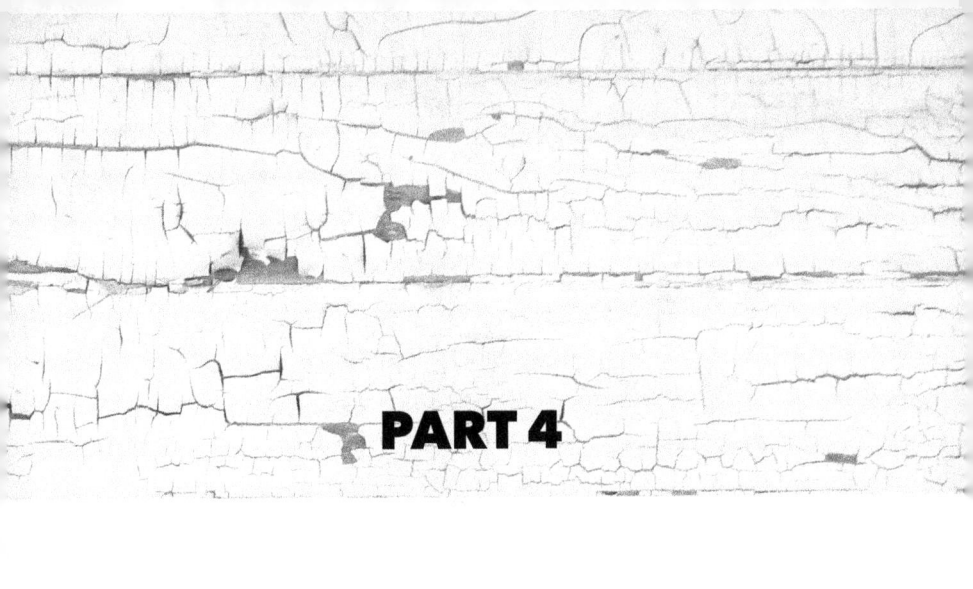

# ABIDING IN THE SAFETY OF GOD'S SECRET PLACE

# CHAPTER 16

# KEEPING YOUR SOUL SECURE IN GOD

Have you ever played hide-and-seek? If so, you can probably recall your favorite hiding place where you felt safe and secure and thought no one would be able to find you. I wasn't so good at this game; I would try to hide in that so-called secret place where I didn't think anyone would be able to find me, but they always did. What is that secret place here that the 91st Psalm alludes to? And what does it mean to abide in the secret place of the Most High?

## THEOLOGICAL BACKGROUND OF THE SECRET PLACE (THE 91ST PSALM)

Notice the very first verse of Psalm 91 (KJV): "He who dwells in the secret place of the Most High shall abide under the shadow of the Almighty." To be in anyone's shadow is to be in their presence. When I was a teenager, my friends and I would play on this certain basketball court in a park that was at the end of the street I lived on. We remember how much fun we had playing basketball together on that court, but we also remember how hot it was in the summertime. We would sweat bullets because the basketball court didn't have any shade, but whenever we took a break and rested under the shade of the trees in the park, we remember how soothing and comforting the shade was for us.

It is possible the author of Psalm 91 wrote verse 1 in reference to the secret place of the Old Testament Tabernacle and Temple, as the verse again says: "He who dwells in the secret place of the Most High, shall abide under the shadows of the Almighty" (Psalms 91:1, KJV). Solomon's Temple was massive and beautiful, and its layout consisted of three areas:

- **The Outer Court:** The outer court is where the children of Israel would gather along with the priest and offer animal sacrifices and worship.
- **The Holy Place:** The Temple had a building in the middle of the outer court that only the priest could enter to perform their priestly duties, which had two areas: the holy place where the priest would burn incense and perform their priestly duties and the Most Holy place.
- **The Most Holy Place (Holy of Holies):** The room furthest back of the Temple was the Most Holy Place, or the Holy of Holies. This place had a curtain (veil) covering the entrance. Only the high priest could enter through the curtain once a year to make atonement on the mercy seat.

In the Most Holy place of Solomon's Temple, there were two giant golden cherubim fifteen feet tall and with wings that touched each other, outstretched seven and a half feet wide. I would imagine that it was an awesome sight whenever the High Priest entered through the curtain into the Most Holy place once a year to make atonement, overshadowed by the two giant cherubim with outstretched wings. There was something significant about the decoration and figures of the cherubim that were inside both the Old Testament Tabernacle and Temple.

If you could look inside the Old Testament Tabernacle, you would notice the curtains (see Exodus 26:1) and carved walls and doors were decorated with cherubim (see 1 Kings 6:29, 31-31). Cherubim also adorned the curtain that covered the entrance to the Most Holy Place. And of course, in the Most Holy Place, two cherubim figures were sculpted out of the mercy seat (see Exodus 25:17-22), and two cherubim stood in the Most Holy place (see 2 Chronicles 3:11). What is the significance of all the decorations and cherubims in the Old Testament Tabernacle and Temple?

Cherubims are depicted as these mighty heavenly guardians of God's throne, presence, and holiness the first time we come across them in the Bible. That's why God placed cherubim eastward of the Garden of Eden after Adam and Eve sinned and were kicked out—to guard the way to the Tree of Life (see Genesis 3:25). God is a Holy God who cannot bear or tolerate sin in His presence, so He placed cherubim there to guard and keep Adam and Eve from accessing the Tree of Life lest they should forever live in their sinful condition and no longer have access to the presence of God like they did before they sinned.

Since that time, the Old Testament priest would serve as the mediator between God and man; people did not have direct access to God in the Old Testament after Adam and Eve lost it. Only the High Priest could enter that so-called secret place—that is, the Most Holy place—once a year to make atonement on the mercy seat of the ark of the covenant, which was like a physical symbol of God's throne, presence, and holiness. And so again, cherubim are depicted in the Bible as these mighty heavenly creatures whose ministry is to guard the throne, presence, and holiness of God. That's why God is described as riding upon a cherub (see Psalms 18:1) and dwelling between cherubim (see Psalms 80:1; Psalms 99:1; Isaiah 37:16). In Exodus 25:22, God tells Moses that He would meet with Him above the mercy seat and would speak to him between the cherubim. It's even possible that Lucifer was a cherubim before his fall from heaven. Ezekiel refers to the anointed cherub who covers (see Ezekiel 28:14), a possible reference to Lucifer as if to say: "You were supposed to cover Me in heaven, not try to steal all of my praise and worship!"

If Adam and Eve (or anyone else) had tried going back into the Garden of Eden to eat from the Tree of Life in their sinful condition, cherubim probably would've hacked them in two with the flaming sword (see Genesis 3:25). But the good news is that when Christ died, that same curtain that covered the Holy of Holies (see 2 Chronicles 3:14) was supernaturally ripped in two (see Matthew 27:51)! What is the significance of the cherubim-decorated curtain—the same curtain that covered the Holy of Holies—supernaturally ripping when Christ died? It was like Christ commanded the cherubim at His death: "You don't have to guard and keep people from the Tree of Life anymore!

You don't have to guard and keep people from the presence of God anymore, because through me, I've made the way for them; through my death, burial, and resurrection, I give them the right to the Tree of Life; I give them access to the presence of God!!" And through Christ, that is why we can come boldly and confidently to His throne of grace, to find mercy and grace to help in time of need (see Hebrews 4:16)!!

Notice again what the psalmist says here in verse 1: "He who dwells in the secret place of the Most High, shall abide in the shadows of the Almighty." The word dwell here comes from the Hebrew word "*yashab*," which denotes inhabiting or taking residence in something as if you're living in it. It's the very same meaning of the word "abide" when Jesus says, "If you abide in me, and my words abide in you, you can ask what you will" (John 15:7, author paraphrase). Jesus was saying, "Stay connected to me, stay in close communication, fellowship, and relationship with me; don't fall away from me or abandon me!" In the Old Testament, that secret place, the Holy of Holies, represented that most intimate place of closeness and communion with God.

**The secret place of the Most High is not so much a physical place as it is a lifestyle**, where we have that intimate closeness and fellowship with God. How are we able to do that practically? Allow me to share a practical, non-exhaustive list of essential practices to apply in order to abide in the secret place of the Most High and live in that place of intimate communion, fellowship, and relationship with God.

# CHAPTER 17

# PRACTICAL APPLICATION #1: A STRONG PRAYER LIFE

The Bible says men ought always to pray and not faint (see Luke 18:1), to pray without ceasing (see 1 Thessalonians 5:16), and the effectual fervent prayer of a righteous man (or woman) is powerful and effective (see James 5:16)! **One of the main ways to have intimacy and fellowship with God is through prayer.** A prayer life is for communion and relationship with God; therefore, we maintain an intimate closeness to God through a strong prayer life.

Kanye West came out with a song some years ago, titled "Jesus Walks," and there's a verse that says: "I wanna to talk to God but I'm afraid because we ain't spoke in so long."[1] In essence, "My prayer life is lacking. I don't have a prayer life!"

---

1  Kanye West, vocalist, "Jesus Walks" by Kanye West, Che Smith, Miri Ben-Ari, and Curtis Lunday, May 25, 2004, track 7 on *The College Dropout*, Roc-A-Fella.

Prayer is talking to God. It's clear from the scriptures above and even others that God intends and desires for us to pray and talk to Him, and He also desires to talk to us; therefore, He intends for us to have a prayer life—a lifestyle of it! My cousin is a minister who often says, "You need prayer, just like you need air!" Prayer is so much more—or it ought to be so much more—than coming to God with our wish list of wants and needs, only when it is convenient for us. Not that we shouldn't give our desires to God because He encourages us to pray and ask Him for what we need and even what we want according to His will. Philippians 4:6-7 says: "Be anxious for nothing but in everything by prayer and supplication, with thanksgiving, let your requests be made known to God." First John 5:14 says that if we ask anything according to God's will, He hears us and we have the petition that we desire of Him" (author paraphrase). So, God encourages us to make our requests known to Him in prayer, but at the same time, a prayer life is more than just making requests; it's about having a lifestyle of communion and intimate fellowship with God.

## OBSERVATIONS OF JESUS' PRAYER LIFE

It is a good practice to pray how Jesus prayed. At times, He shut out everything for personal, intimate communion and fellowship with God in prayer (see Matthew 14:23; Mark 1:35, 6:46; Luke 5:16).

You may close your eyes when you pray and likely see others close their eyes in church. Why do we do that? We close our eyes as a gesture of reverence to God and shut everything out so we can give Him our undivided attention. We see this in Luke 5:16. Jesus closed His eyes in prayer, and He did it often. He laid

## PRACTICAL APPLICATION #1: A STRONG PRAYER LIFE

His business aside, withdrew from the crowds, and spent time in solitude for uninterrupted communion and fellowship with His Heavenly Father in prayer. This practice allows us to offer God our complete focus and attention. It gives us a heightened experience of close communion and fellowship with God so that we may hear God more clearly. Sometimes the reason why we may not hear God clearly isn't because He doesn't desire to speak, but because of the clutter in our lives, our minds, and our thoughts. That clutter could be sin or a lackluster approach to prayer where we just go through the motions as our mind is consumed by five or ten different things, or we are trying to juggle five or ten different things at the same time. In these moments, God is saying: "Where is the reverence? I am God, and I want to commune with you; I want to speak to you!" Ice Cube once said to Dr. Dre: "Yo, Dre! I got something to say!" I don't know if God would say "yo!" but He does say that He wants to speak to you and commune with you, but your mind is on too many other things. This compromises what communion and fellowship with God ought to look like in prayer.

Prayer is spending quality, uninterrupted time with God to refresh and renew us into a richer relationship with Him. For me, it only takes one day to feel the difference between days when I don't prioritize prayer and days when I do. I get it; sometimes it can be challenging, especially when our daily routines keep us busy. We're always on the go and can get so occupied with things like excessive time on our phones, iPads, computers, TV, Facebook, Twitter—you name it—not to mention work, activities, and our relationships. These distractions and obligations can catapult us into dry seasons of prayer. If **we are too busy to spend** time with God in prayer, then we're too busy! That happens to me sometimes. I can get so busy that I don't commune with God like I ought to. God convicts me and I repent with, "God, I am sorry, something has gotta go, and it's not going to be my time with you!" The passage in Luke is a wake-up call, because Jesus was busier than we could ever be, but He still always managed to prioritize prayer because **He knew the effectiveness of His ministry and everything He did was tied to the effectiveness of His prayer life and communion with God.** He prioritized His prayer life to maximize His ministry.

When our prayer life is healthy, we will meet and encounter God. When our prayer life isn't healthy, we go through the motions but do not meet or encounter God.

I heard someone once ask: "If God knows everything, if He knows what we need before we even ask, if He is all powerful and sees everything happening in the world, if He knows what He's going to do before He does it, then why then do we need to pray?" You'll find the answer to that question in the Bible.

## THE ESSENTIALS OF A STRONG PRAYER LIFE

Matthew 6:5-15 is a foundational text where Jesus teaches the essentials of and reasons to foster a healthy prayer life. In Matthew, Jesus teaches us how to pray. In Matthew 6:5, Jesus first teaches His disciples how *not* to pray. He starts by saying that when you pray (not if you pray), already emphasizing our need for a lifestyle of prayer.

During Jesus' time, especially hypocritical religious leaders such as the Pharisees prayed just to be seen, and people still do that today. They prayed with the wrong motives. They cared

## PRACTICAL APPLICATION #1: A STRONG PRAYER LIFE

more about impressing, so Jesus discouraged that kind of prayer and even went as far as to say that those religious leaders had already received their greatest reward—being seen (see Matthew 6:5). Now it's important to note that Jesus was not condemning public or corporate prayer, because God also encourages us to pray together. Corporate prayer is another essential of a strong prayer life—praying together with one another, as Jesus tells us in Matthew 18:19-20 (NIV), "Again, truly I tell you that if two of you on earth agree about anything they ask for, it will be done for them by my Father in heaven, for where two or three [and more] gather in my name, there am I with them." So, that scripture and many others encourage us to pray together with one another. But in Matthew 6, Jesus addresses the *motive* behind praying, that if you pray for the purpose of being seen, you pray with the wrong motive. God will manifest the rewards of our prayer life, and it will speak for itself (see Matthew 6:6).

In Matthew 6:7, Jesus also warns them about using vain, long-winded repetitions or words just to sound impressive. Jesus discourages His followers and disciples from praying in that fashion because it doesn't create communion with God. God doesn't hear those prayers. It doesn't matter to God how long or short our prayers are. He just wants us to be real; He's not looking for fancy speech or big words. He wants us to talk to Him from our hearts; He wants us to be genuine and sincere when we pray. So, Jesus starts with some pointers on how not to pray and then reiterates it in Matthew 6:8. Finally, in Matthew 6:9-13, Jesus teaches us how to pray.

Matthew 6:9-13 is known to be the "template" for praying to God because it has all the essentials of a healthy prayer life.

## A REFLECTION ON THE PRIVILEGE OF PRAYER

It's a wonderful privilege to commune with and talk to God who created you and everything in the heavens and on earth through prayer. We get to pray to the One who holds all things and all power in His hands, the One who is all-knowing and knows you better than you even know yourself. What a privilege it is to know that He desires to hear from you and talk back!

*What is the purpose of a lifestyle of prayer, and why should we pray?*

To answer this question, we need to reference a foundational text in Matthew 6:5-15 and Revelation 3:20.

**1) Because God desires to commune with us.**

God desires to have fellowship and a relationship with us, and a strong prayer life facilitates that relationship. In the Bible, communion carries the idea of an intimate fellowship, sharing, and even partnership. In Revelation 3:20, Jesus says: "If anyone opens the door I will come in and eat with him and him with Me" (author paraphrase). That's communion; that's sharing; that's fellowship! We can also incorporate praise, worship, and thanksgiving in our prayer life, and we will see the manifestation and work of God come to life. The Bible talks about how Daniel had an excellent spirit (see Daniel 5:12, 6:3). Daniel was in a foreign land, and the king Nebuchadnezzar even gave Him a Babylonian name because he wanted Daniel and the other captive Jews to adopt and take on the Babylonian culture, but Daniel remained faithful to God and so God brought him favor. As a result, Daniel excelled. He was effective in everything he did and all his spheres of influence because he was a praying man (see Daniel 6:10). A strong prayer life will permeate God's blessing into every area of your life. It all goes back to what Jesus said in Matthew 6:6 (author paraphrase): "My Father who sees you praying in secret will reward you openly."

**2) Because prayer gives us a proper perspective of God and who He is.**

We see this in the beginning of Jesus' prayer when He says: "Our Father which art in heaven, hallowed be thy name" (Matthew 6:9, KJV). Jesus began His prayers with a proper perspective of who God is ("Our Father which art in heaven") and acknowledged God for who He is ( "hallowed [holy] is your name"). Even Proverbs 3:5-6 says, "Trust in the LORD with all your heart and lean not to your own understanding; in all your ways **acknowledge Him** and He shall direct your paths." Acknowledging God not only means seeking Him for guidance, but recognizing and acknowledging God for who He is. If we're not careful, we can pray as if our circumstances and problems are bigger than God, but when we pray like that, God says, "Do you know who I am!? I am God!" When we commune with and pray to God, we ought to pray like we know who God is. It helps to think about all God has done for you. When you also look at other examples of people who prayed in the Bible, they always began their prayers with a proper perspective and recognition of God and even acknowledged and praised Him for who He is. For example, when you look at Daniel's prayer in the Bible (see Daniel 9:1-23), he begins his prayer with: "O Lord, great and awesome God, who keeps His covenant and mercy with those who love Him and obey His commandments" (v. 4). Daniel began his prayer with a proper perspective and recognition of God, acknowledging and praising God for His greatness and faithfulness to His covenant. When

King Jehoshaphat prayed, Israel was facing invading armies in 2 Chronicles 20:6. He began with: "O LORD, God of our fathers, are you not God in heaven? You rule over all the kingdoms of the nations. In your hand are power and might, so that none is able to withstand you" (ESV). Once again, this prayer begins a proper perspective and recognition of God and acknowledges God for who He is (i.e., Lord, God of Heaven, ruler over all kingdoms and nations, sovereign power and might).

How do you acknowledge God in your prayers? Only you can acknowledge and speak of who God is according to your personal relationship with Him and experience of Him (i.e., the truth of who God is in your life, who He is as revealed in the scriptures, etc.). For example, sometimes when I pray to God, I declare how wonderful and awesome and mighty He is. Why? Because I have seen and experienced God at work in my own life in wonderful, awesome, and mighty ways. I have known and experienced God as a provider whenever I've needed something from Him. So, I may say something like: "God, you are my source and my provider; you meet and supply all of my needs." Whenever I was sick and needed to recover, I knew God as a healer. I often begin my prayers with: "God, you are my Healer, You are my source of healing who is able to heal all things." When God has redeemed and delivered me from something (e.g., a sin or a situation), I acknowledge and praise God for His redemption and deliverance.

**3) Because prayer brings us into alignment with God's will so that it manifests in our lives and in the world.**

Prayer is not just a wish list of things we want God to do. We aren't to treat God as some genie who will grant our every wish and desire. Prayer doesn't change God; prayer changes things and changes us! As I've mentioned, one element of communion with God is our partnership with Him—where we partner with God, not where He partners with our program. No, we partner with God's program, and truly genuine prayer where we request God's will to be done will align us with His will. The next line of Jesus' prayer says, "Thy kingdom come. Thy will be done in earth, as *it is* in heaven" (Matthew 6:10, KJV). Here, Jesus is asking and praying for God's will to be done on earth as it is in heaven, by God's power and authority (His kingdom), because in heaven everything is in perfect alignment with God's will. I once heard a fellow ask: "If God knows everything and has all power, why do we even need to pray? Couldn't God just say 'zap!' and do as He wishes?" Yes of course! God does know everything past, present, and future and has all the power in His hands to do as He wishes, even without our prayers. However, **GOD HAS CHOSEN prayer as a means to activate His will in the world and our own lives,** and that's why God's Word is filled with scriptures that exhort us to pray—men ought always to pray and not faint (see Luke 18:1); "pray without ceasing" (1 Thessalonians 5:17). Throughout the Bible, we clearly see that God is both a prayer-hearing and a prayer-answering God and encourages us to ask and pray for His will to be done (see Matthew 6:10; John 14:13, 15:7; 1 John 5:14). **Therefore, prayer aligns us with God's providence.**

### God's Miracles and Providence

If God has ever done a miracle in your life, you might think of God's miracles as defying circumstances and events to accomplish His will. Perhaps you have experienced an event with no natural explanation or logic. You knew it had to be a miracle. God's providence works in our circumstances to accomplish His will in our lives. The Bible speaks to God's providence. For example, Romans 8:28 speaks of God governing and orchestrating circumstances and events in our lives—even bad ones—to accomplish His will to work for our good. I can imagine that Joseph had some intense conversations with God. "God, what's happening to me now? Where I am? This isn't what you showed me! This isn't what it is supposed to look like!" Through his dreams, God revealed to Joseph that he would be a ruler (see Genesis 37:5-11), but not before his brothers would hate him (see Genesis 37:4). They threw him into a pit and sold him into slavery (see Genesis 38:18-28). He was falsely accused and thrown in prison (see Genesis 39). Yet after years passed, Joseph's brothers recognized him as the prime minister of Egypt (the ruler God had shown him in his dreams), second in command to the Pharaoh. They feared Joseph was going to get revenge on them for what they did (see Genesis 50:17-18), but Joseph forgave his brothers and recognized God's providence when he said: "Don't be afraid. . . . you meant evil against me; *but* God meant it for good" (Genesis 50:19-20). At some point, Joseph recognized God's providence at work in his life, even through the bad and unpleasant circumstances. These experiences got him to the place God wanted him to be (see Genesis 41-46).

In the early 2000s, I graduated from Clemson with a Bachelor of Science degree in electrical engineering. After graduation, I had no idea how hard it would be to find a job out of college. In 2005, I worked at a golf ball plant, the same job I had before I graduated. Many people taunted me, asking me how and why

## PRACTICAL APPLICATION #1: A STRONG PRAYER LIFE

I still worked there with an engineering degree. One guy even told me to my face that I would never be an engineer. In 2006, while I was still looking for an engineering job, I worked on a few projects as a contractor. Contracting can be a cutthroat business; you can be let go at any moment. While working on a project with another guy, I found out they had enough money in their budget to keep only one of us, so they kept the other guy and laid me off. After that, I worked any two jobs I could find for a while just to maintain. I received several criticisms at my jobs, such as, "What in the world are you doing working here with an engineering degree?!" and "You need to go back to school!" or "You must be in the wrong field, or you must not have enough passion!"

Those hurtful comments really tested and challenged me. I was confused and frustrated and discouraged about finding the right career, but God still used people to encourage and remind me of His promises. These reminders also came from prayer and quiet time where I would read and meditate on His Word.

Eventually, as God worked providentially in my life, He opened a door for me at Fluor, an engineering, procurement, and construction (EPC) company in Greenville, SC. It was awesome how God worked and brought me into favor with Fluor. After the first phone interview went well, I was invited to an in-person interview and a tour of the company with the electrical department manager. The HR lady asked me: "How much do you think you should start off with?" I gave her a number for a salary and a few days later she called me back and told me what the electrical department manager said: "Well, we're going to make him really happy; we're going to give him a bigger number!" They nearly doubled the salary I asked for! In less than a year of working at Fluor, I received two big annual raises based on performance. **My prayers and other people God used to encourage and pray for me helped me to realize and align myself with God's providence at work in my life and gave Him the praise, glory, and honor.** I knew that it was God who worked all things together for my good (see Romans 8:28).

**4) Because prayer keeps us humble and dependent on God.**

The next statement that Jesus makes in His prayer is: "Give us this day our daily bread." Now think about this. If God gave us everything we ever needed at once, do you honestly think we would seek God and pray to Him consistently or depend on Him like we ought to? Probably not. This part of Jesus' prayer conveys that prayer and dependence on God is a daily exercise (not once in a while or when it's convenient for us). No, we should pray and depend on God *daily* to give us what we need and sustain us. Jesus then prays: "Lead us not into temptation, but deliver us from the evil one" (Matthew 6:13, NIV). This request encourages us to humbly seek and depend on God the Heavenly Father for guidance, direction, and protection. Each morning, I pray and depend on God to lead and guide me throughout the day. I ask for God's wisdom, guidance, direction, and protection, as He knows what the day has in store for all of us.

## When and How Often Should We Pray?

We should pray at least daily, especially in the mornings before we start our daily routines. The writer of Psalm 63:1 says, "Early will I seek you, my soul thirst after you and longs for you" (author paraphrase). Every morning, we need God to pour into us and fill us, and a lot of times we may not always have the discipline

## PRACTICAL APPLICATION #1: A STRONG PRAYER LIFE

that we need. Throughout your day, make it a habit to stop or set aside time to pray. When we pray in the mornings, we meet with God; we encounter God, and we can begin to walk with God before we meet the devil or anything else we may face that day. Praying and communing with God in the morning will set the tone for your day and invite God's providence to work in your life. I know schedules and routines can complicate it. There was a time when I worked all night shifts, and I slept for a good part of the morning into the afternoon. But once I got up and before I started my routine, I prayed. I've looked back many times and realized that some things didn't happen by mere chance or coincidence but by God's providence. I daily sought the Lord, asked Him to order my steps, asked Him to lead and guide me throughout the day, and asked for His will to be done and accomplished in my life. So, the mornings are generally a good time to pray and seek Him, and the scriptures also support this (see Psalms 63:1; Mark 1:35).

Now, do we *have* to pray in the mornings? No, not necessarily, but it's simply a good practice and a way to show God that we are seeking Him first and making Him our first priority. However, we can pray multiple times throughout the day (we see Daniel praying three times a day in Daniel 6:10), as Jesus says men ought to always pray and not faint (or give up; see Luke 18:1). Similarly, the Apostle Paul says to "pray without ceasing" (1 Thessalonians 5:17). So, my prayer time doesn't have to end in the mornings; that's just when it begins. I pray in my car and my cubicle at work. I whisper things to Him that I need help with. Praying to God should be both daily and continuous.

## 5) Because prayer helps us to maintain a close fellowship and relationship with God.

Next, Jesus says, "Forgive us our debts as we forgive our debtors." Praying to God daily and continually helps us to maintain a close fellowship and relationship with God, specifically by confession and repentance of our sins. Unconfessed and unrepentant sin puts a wedge between us and God (see Isaiah 59:2), but when we confess our sins, the Bible says that God "is faithful and just to forgive us *our* sins and to cleanse us from all unrighteousness" (1 John 1:9). We also see the importance of forgiving those who have wronged or sinned against us so that we can receive God's forgiveness when we need it and ask for it (see Matthew 6:12). Unforgiveness can also put a wedge between us and God; if we don't forgive others, God will not forgive us (see Matthew 6:14). Now that doesn't mean we would go to hell. If you're a Christian and have unforgiveness in your heart toward someone, God is still your Heavenly Father, and you're still His daughter or son, so who you are to Him won't change—it's your fellowship and communion with God that will change.

After Jesus asked God for what He needed, He ended by acknowledging and affirming who God is: "For Yours is the kingdom and the power and the glory forever. Amen" (Matthew 6:13).

## The Method of Prayer

What does it mean to ask and pray in Jesus' name? Will God give us whatever it is we ask for? Can we come to God with a wish list and simply tack on the magic ending phrase, "in Jesus' name," and assume He'll do it for us? Can we use the name of Jesus like a genie in a bottle, granting our every wish and command? **The short answer to all these questions is no! We can't!** If we're not careful, we might understand and approach prayer in that way. For instance, there's a theological school of thought called "Name it, claim it!" which is typical of "prosperity preaching" and even of the "word of faith" and "new age" movements. "Name it, claim it" is a philosophy that uses the power of your faith to create your own reality and get whatever you want. There's a big problem with "Name it, claim it," because our faith is only as good as the object of what we place our faith in. We can believe and have faith in something all day long, but if our faith is not based on the right thing (i.e., God and His Word), then it is futile faith.

In the gospel of John 13-17, Jesus spent His final moments with His disciples in the upper room prior to His crucifixion, and it wouldn't be long before He returned back to the Heavenly Father in eternal glory. Before His departure, Jesus left His disciples with the privilege of asking and praying to the Heavenly Father for things in His name. Asking for things in Jesus' name was never intended to be to control or manipulate God into giving us whatever we want, but **there *is* a purpose in asking and praying in His name.** In the gospel of John 14:13, Jesus says: "Whatever you ask in my name, that I will do, that the Father may be glorified in the Son." The ultimate purpose of praying to God the Father in Jesus' name is to glorify God in the Son. In other words, when we genuinely ask and pray to God in the name of Jesus, God will move, act, and answer our prayers **for His glory**. Jesus adds, "so that your joy may be full" (John 16:24, NASB). There's great joy in answered prayer, and the key to answered prayers is prayers prayed in the name of Jesus. How do we pray in the name of Jesus, and what does that really mean? There are four things to consider when you pray in Jesus' name.

- **To pray in Jesus' name means we approach God on the basis of Jesus' merit rather than our own.**

None of us can approach God on the basis of our own merit, goodness, or works, because our righteousness is as filthy rags before God (see Isaiah 64:6) and we don't have any goodness or merit (self-righteousness) of our own as we approach God (see Psalm 14:1-3). However, we can approach God and come boldly to His throne of grace in prayer only because of the goodness, merit, and works of Jesus Christ (see Hebrews 4:15-16). Jesus Christ made the way for us, bridging the gap between us and God by His blood. Therefore, God is faithful to hear and answer the prayers that we pray in Jesus Christ's name.

- **To pray in Jesus' name means we ask and pray for things that are in line with God's will.**

First John 5:14 (NASB) says: "This is the confidence which we have before Him [God], that, if we ask anything according to His will, He hears us. And if we know that He hears us *in* whatever we ask, we know that we have the requests which we have asked from Him."

## CHAPTER 18

# PRACTICAL APPLICATION #2: FASTING

Why should we fast? You'll notice in the Gospel of Matthew 6:16 that Jesus did not say, "If you fast;" He said, "*When you fast.*" Just like praying, fasting should be a part of our spiritual discipline. In this passage, Jesus first taught how *not* to fast—to show off or be seen like the Pharisees. The Pharisees were one of the religious Jewish groups, who, among other things, often prayed and fasted to appear to have a form of godliness, but their hearts were far from God (see Matthew 15:1-8). Jesus warned His followers to avoid fasting for show (like the Pharisees). So, why *should* we fast?

You have probably heard the phrase "less is more." What do people mean when they say that? Sometimes less of something can greatly benefit or increase something else. For example, if a person spends less money, they could save more or give more. The same is true of fasting; it's a spiritual discipline that requires denying ourselves of something (having less or none). Food is the most classic example. When we go without food for a period of time, we experience God in a greater, deeper, and more intimate way. The Bible says that God rewards those who diligently seek Him (see Matthew 6:18; Hebrews 11:6). Therefore, fasting is a spiritual discipline where we shift our focus from physical things, desires, and pleasures onto God. **When God has our sincere focus and attention, we are put in a position to experience Him in a greater, deeper, and more intimate way (see Hebrews 11:6).**

Very often fasting is associated with prayer (see Acts 13:3, 14:23). The purpose of fasting is to have a mindset of focus on God. We focus on God through reciprocal dialog. We take time to talk and share our hearts with God, and we also take time to listen and hear from God, so fasting is blessed when we pair it with prayer. People in the Bible often worshipped during their fasts (see Acts 13:2). Other times, fasting was associated with sadness (see 2 Samuel 1:12), repentance of sin (see Joel 2:12-13), and/or humbling yourself before God (see Psalm 69:10-12).

How should you fast? People who fasted in the Bible generally fasted from food for a period of time. For example, you may choose to skip a meal during the day or refrain from certain foods like Daniel did. Because of Daniel's commitment, he experienced God in a great and mighty way (see Daniel 1:12, 10:2-3). I do believe that fasting is not limited strictly to food. Many things are good for us to fast, like social media. Fasting from social media for a period of time re-routes our focus to God. If you're always on the computer, your iPad, or your iPhone, it'll probably do you some good to lay them aside for a little while to focus more on God and experience more of Him. If you like watching TV like I do, it may do you some good to cut the TV off temporarily and focus more on Him so that you may experience Him. **There's something about a quiet place where we can hear God more clearly and experience more of Him because He has our undivided focus and attention.** It's a blessed experience! Therefore, we can find intimate communion and fellowship with God through fasting (along with prayer, worship, etc.)

## CHAPTER 19

# PRACTICAL APPLICATION #3: GENUINE AND TRUE WORSHIP

We also maintain intimate communion and fellowship with God through our worship of Him. Our worship to God is our loving response to Him. It gives Him honor, reverence, respect, adoration, praise, and glory because of who He is and what He has done for us by His love.

In the Bible, God says to His chosen people in Exodus 20:1 (author paraphrase): "I am the Lord Your God, who brought you out of Egypt, out of the place of slavery, therefore, you are not to have any other gods before me." That was the very first commandment that God gave to Israel. In other words, because of who God is and what He did in His covenant relationship to Israel as their Lord, Redeemer, and Deliverer who was faithful to the covenant promise He made, the correct response was to worship Him and only Him. God often warned His people about making or worshiping idols (see Exodus 20:4).

The Bible says that God is a jealous God (see Exodus 34:14), yet God's jealousy is not jealousy as we understand it. We typically think of jealousy as envying someone who might have something that we do not have or who might have something that we want, but God isn't jealous in that sense. God is self-sufficient. He doesn't need anything from us. God is a jealous God in that He desires and wants what is rightfully His, which is our worship, and whenever we take something that is rightfully God's and gives it to something or someone else (i.e., an idol), He becomes jealous. Beyond this, God is jealous for us whom He loves; God wants us to experience all the fullness of His love, His goodness, and His best He wants to show us who He is!

*It's tempting to worship idols instead of depend on and trust in God.*

Jesus says: "Blessed *are* those who hunger and thirst after righteousness, For they shall be filled." Matthew 5:6. This verse speaks to the void, longing, hunger, or thirst inside of us that only God can truly fill, satisfy, and quench. Righteousness means to be in right standing with God, but it also means trusting and depending on God. It's allowing God's will and Word to govern us so that our needs will be satisfied in His way. When we look to something (or someone) other than God to fill the void (or need) that only He can fill or try and fulfill a legitimate God-given need in an ungodly or illegitimate way, we are tempted into idol worship.

## PRACTICAL APPLICATION #3: GENUINE AND TRUE WORSHIP

Israel was tempted to worship idols. Look at what the prophet Isaiah says concerning Israel: "Those who trust in carved idols will be turned back, And utterly put to shame" (Isaiah 43:17, AMP).

Idols may give a false sense of hope, but they cannot truly satisfy or give us what only God can give. As God spoke through the prophet Isaiah, putting our hope and trust in idols will set us up for disappointment (put us to shame).

When you study the history of Israel and God's chosen people in the Bible, particularly in the Old Testament, you will find that idol worship was one of Israel's greatest struggles and temptations. God often warned and even judged Israel for idolatry. Even today, we find ourselves tempted to worship an idol or idols, because we all have a vacancy inside of us that we try to fill, and we'll either fill it with God or something else. **An idol can be anything or anyone that we love more than God and/or even worship in the place of God. When we look to anything or anyone else to fill the void in our lives that only God can fill, we are guilty of idol worship.**

Corporate worship is the gathering of saints for worship on a Sunday or any other day. Giving your voice and time, lifting your hands, and singing praises of adoration to God for who He is and what He's done for you are all gestures of worship. But worship is more than just a gesture or gestures because people with hearts far from God can do all those things, and that's how Jesus referred to the hypocritical religious leaders of His day. He said, "These people draw near to Me with their mouth, And honor Me with *their* lips, But their heart is far from me" (Matthew 15:8). Both Cain and Abel made gestures of worship to God through their offerings, but the Bible says that Abel's offering was pleasing to God while Cain's was not (see Genesis 4:4-5) because Cain's heart and attitude towards God were not right. **We cannot genuinely experience intimate communion with God through our worship unless our hearts and attitudes are right with Him and other people.** For example, a person who harbors hatred, bitterness, unforgiveness, or the like towards someone cannot experience genuine intimacy and closeness to God through their worship until they first get their heart and attitude issues resolved (see Genesis 4:7; Matthew 5:23-24).

In John 4, Jesus tells the Samaritan woman that "the hour is coming and is now here, when the true worshipers will worship the Father in spirit and truth" (John 4:23, ESV). **True worship is our genuine response to God from our spirit and is based on the revelation of the truth of who He is and all that He's done, as revealed in the scriptures.** Genuine worship of God is not confined only to a gesture, a religious deed or action, or a particular location, time, or day. Rather, **our very lifestyle should be a response of honor, reverence, and adoration to God for who He is and all that He has done for us!**

God desires us to worship Him with our whole being, as Deuteronomy 6:5 says, "Love the LORD your God with all your heart, with all your soul, and with all your strength." God doesn't want just a part of you; He wants all of you. Let's consider a final point about worship. Paul says in Romans 12:1 (NASB), "Therefore I urge you, brothers *and sisters*, by the mercies of God, to present your bodies as a living and holy sacrifice, acceptable to God, *which is* your spiritual service of worship." The proper response to the riches of His grace, His promises, His blessings, His benefits, and His privileges is to worship Him. We are to present ourselves as a living sacrifice with a lifestyle of honor, reverence, and adoration to God. We are to allow God to use us and do whatever He desires to do in and through our lives for His honor and glory!

# CHAPTER 20

# PRACTICAL APPLICATION #4: GENUINE PRAISE

Praise is one of many forms of worship. We can experience closeness and intimacy with God when our praise is genuine and sincere, and He will respond to it. When I praise God, there are times when I feel His love and presence in such a way that causes me to cry happy tears. His presence overwhelms me as I think about who He is in my life, His goodness, His love, His faithfulness, and all He's done for me. The Book of Psalms is all about praising God. You'll find the phrase, "Praise the Lord!" in many of the psalms. This phrase is translated from the Hebrew verb "Hallelujah," which is an emphatic command to bestow "bragging," "boasting," and "honor" to God. As I mentioned in a previous chapter, my favorite athlete growing up 90s was Michael Jordan. During my very brief basketball aspirations in school, I tried to play ball and make moves on the playground court just like Michael Jordan. Whenever I saw him play, I was always in awe of the great skill, athleticism, and artistry he demonstrated on the basketball court, whether it was lighting up the New York Knicks in a playoff game, his strong will to push through sickness during game five of the 1997 NBA finals against the Utah Jazz, or his iconic crossover of Byron Russell in which he made the final shot with seconds left, winning the Chicago Bulls the sixth NBA championship. Since the Bulls were my favorite basketball team, I would brag and boast about Michael Jordan to my friends and all he did and accomplished on the basketball court. While praising God is bragging and boasting about God, it is also honoring God. God desires our praise; He desires for us to brag and boast and honor Him for who He is and all that He's done for us.

When we brag and boast about God and how great He is, God will respond to us and others in kind (see 2 Corinthians 20:21; Acts 16:25).

Second Chronicles 20 details the history of King Jehoshaphat at a time when multiple foreign armies invaded in an effort to overthrow the kingdom of Israel. The king knew he was outnumbered and didn't have a strategy or plan for fighting against these foreign armies, so he turned to God and prayed. In response, God promised that He would fight for Israel and be with them, and the people would see the salvation of God. On the following day, when Israel moved against the foreign armies, King Jehoshaphat did an odd thing—he appointed singers of the people of Israel to praise God as they went out before the foreign armies (see 2 Chronicles 20:21-22). Notice what God did and how He responded to the praise.

## PRACTICAL APPLICATION #4: GENUINE PRAISE

*And when he had consulted with the people, he appointed singers unto the LORD, and* **that should praise the beauty of holiness,** *as they went out before the army, and to say,* **Praise the LORD; for his mercy** *endureth* **for ever. And when they began to sing and to praise, the LORD set ambushments against the children of Ammon, Moab, and mount Seir, which were come against Judah; and they were smitten.**—*KJV (author emphasis added)*

When the people of Israel sang praises to God, God revealed His greatness, fighting off the foreign armies that came against Israel by setting ambushes against them. When we experience darkness and hopelessness and don't know what to pray for, our praise can be the prayer that God answers. He will respond to our praise by showing Himself great and mighty as He works in that dark and hopeless situation (see 2 Corinthians 19:21; Acts 16:25). Nothing is too hard for God!

# CHAPTER 21

# PRACTICAL APPLICATION #5: ABIDING IN CHRIST

To abide in that secret place of the Most High, we also need to abide in Christ. It is Christ who made it possible for us to approach God and enter that secret place to experience intimate communion, fellowship, and relationship with God. In John 15:4, Jesus charged His disciples to: "Abide in Me, and I in you, As the branch cannot bear fruit of itself, unless it abides in the vine, neither can you, unless you abide in Me." In verses 7 and 8, Jesus says: "If you abide in Me, and My words abide in you, you will ask what you desire, and it shall be done for you. By this My Father is glorified, that you bear much fruit, so you will be my disciples." As mentioned before, to abide means to stay or to remain. Jesus identifies Himself as the vine and His disciples as the branches to warn them not to abandon or fall away from

Him, but to instead remain faithful and committed to Him! There are many examples of people who were alleged followers of Jesus but later abandoned Him or fell away from Him because they were not genuinely faithful or committed to following Him in the first place. In so many words, Jesus was telling His disciples: "Don't be like them. You remain. You abide in me, be steadfast in me, and remain faithful and committed to me!"

He never promises that His followers will have an easy or convenient life. Many things can and will happen in our lives. All of us will face difficult issues and problems, like the death of a loved one, losing a job or relationship, sadness, disappointments, heartbreak, setbacks, anger, frustration, or worry; nevertheless, God's charge to us is that we don't abandon or fall away from following Him but remain faithful and committed to Him. That is the mark of a genuine disciple. In John 15:7, Jesus characterizes a genuine disciple as one who will remain faithful, committed, and connected to God, just like a branch fastens to a vine. The end result is that we will bear much fruit. Fruit is the manifestation of God at work in and through our lives. A branch gets its supply, water, and nutrients from its vine when it remains connected to it and then bears fruit. Similarly, when we abide in Christ, we are connected to the divine source who is God, and His presence and power will be at work in and through our lives to produce fruit in our character, our behavior, our lifestyle, our actions, and in everything we do and accomplish for the glory of God!

# CHAPTER 22

# PRACTICAL APPLICATION #6: CONFESSION AND REPENTANCE OF SIN

We maintain intimate communion and fellowship with God by confessing our sins. The Prophet Isaiah told the people that "the Lord's hand is not shortened that it can't save, neither is His ear dull of hearing, but that their sins have separated them from their God" (Isaiah 59:1, author paraphrase). Sin will break our communion and fellowship with God unlike anything else. **This is why we need to be quick to confess and repent of any sins we are aware of daily.**

## CONFESSION OF SIN

The good news for us is where sin abounds, God's grace abounds more (see Romans 5:20). That means, even if you don't know Christ in the free pardon of your sins, no matter who you are, no matter what you've done, no matter your past, or no matter what you may be doing now, you are not beyond the reach of God's love and grace, even when you feel unworthy of it or like He could never forgive you. His grace and forgiveness are always available to you if you're willing to receive them through Jesus Christ! The Holy Spirit convicts even Christians when we sin or do something that we know is not pleasing to God. We may wrestle with feelings of guilt, shame, and fear when we sin, and in a way, that's a good thing, because we can do something about how we feel. But if we are not careful, those feelings can drive us away from God instead of towards God. That's what happened to Adam and Eve when they sinned. The Bible says their eyes were opened, and they became burdened with feelings of guilt, shame, and fear and tried to run and hide from God (see Genesis 3:8) instead of running toward God.

The thought of anyone trying to run and hide from God might sound funny because God knows everything and sees everything because He's omnipresent. But when we become so burdened with our guilt, shame, and fear and allow them to drive us away from God or isolate ourselves from God because we fear God can't love us or forgive us after what we did, we won't take it to God or talk to Him about it. So, in a sense, we're trying to cover or hide ourselves from God. But God's love for us is unconditional, and God's love for us is not based on our performance. His grace abounds more than our sins! Does God's

## PRACTICAL APPLICATION #6: CONFESSION AND REPENTANCE OF SIN

grace give us a license to sin? No! The Apostle Paul asked: "Shall we continue in sin, that grace may abound?" (Romans 6:1, KJV). The answer, of course, is no! Every genuine Christian has a real desire and intention to live a life that is honorable and pleasing to God and based on His word, but we will still sin because we are housed in this unredeemed body of flesh until the day Jesus comes back.

The Bible says "If we confess our sins, He is faithful and just to forgive us *our* sins and to cleanse us from all unrighteousness (1 John 1:9). Confession means we are open and honest with God about our sin; it means we call it out and confess it as God sees it. There's no need to be shy about it; God already knows anyway. When we sin, when we fail and come short, we just have to be honest with God and confess: "Yes, Lord, I did such and such (fill in the blank). I screwed up," and He will be faithful and just to forgive your sins and cleanse you from all unrighteousness. Sometimes we still wrestle with guilt and shame even after God has forgiven us, as if God's love, grace, and forgiveness are not enough. I struggle with that at times because I love God so much and am passionate about living a life that brings glory and honor to God, so when I fail and fall short of His glory, I take it personally. However, I'm still quick to be honest with God and repent when I do sin. Sometimes I get overwhelmed and teary-eyed thinking about God's grace, goodness, and forgiveness. Even at my worst, God still loves me and desires to use me for His glory. Even at your worst, God still loves you, still has plans for you, still desires to use you, and intends to get the glory!

## REPENTANCE OF SIN

The confession of our sin(s) is an important step in maintaining a close fellowship and relationship with God, yet there is another important step beyond the confession of our sins—genuine repentance. Repentance is "turning away" from sin. It is making a complete turn in the opposite direction from the one you are going.

King David wrote Psalm 51 after God sent the prophet Nathan to confront him about his adultery with Bathsheba and the murder of her husband, Uriah, to try to cover up his sins. Nathan's confrontation shows us that God will confront us one way or another with our sin when we don't and force us to deal with it. We may criticize David for his "big" sin, but despite his failures, God called David a man after His own heart and in this psalm, we see how King David turned to God and called upon His mercy, the same mercy that we all need for our sins. We can see four elements of genuine repentance in Psalm 51.

**1) David's prayer of repentance is an appeal for God's mercy.**

In verse 1, David says: "Have mercy upon me, O God, According to Your lovingkindness; According to the multitude of Your tender mercies."

David knew that He deserved God's judgment for His sin, so he knew forgiveness wouldn't come from his own goodness or merit, but from God's lovingkindness and multitude of his tender mercies. Our righteousness is as filthy rags, but fortunately, on the basis of God's lovingkindness and tender mercies towards us, He is willing to forgive us, wash us, and cleanse us from our sins when we seek His mercy.

## PRACTICAL APPLICATION #6: CONFESSION AND REPENTANCE OF SIN

**2) David's prayer of repentance is an acknowledgment and confession of sin.**

David says, "Blot out my transgressions. Wash me thoroughly from my iniquity, And cleanse me from my sin. For I acknowledge my transgressions, And my sin is always before me. Against You, You only, have I sinned" (vv. 1-4). David acknowledged and confessed his sin before God.

**3) David's prayer of repentance is a genuine desire for a cleansing and changing of the heart.**

Beginning in verse 7, David says, "Purge me with hyssop, and I shall be clean. Wash me, and I shall be whiter than snow;" then in verse 10, he says: "Create in me a clean heart, O God, And renew a steadfast spirit within me." Hyssop was a leafy plant that the Old Testament priest would use to sprinkle blood or water on a person for ceremonial cleansing, like a leper or someone who had touched a dead body. So, David used hyssop as a metaphor; he desired for God to cleanse Him from the defilement of sin from the inside out when he asked God to create in him a clean heart and renew a right spirit within him. **True genuine repentance begins with a genuine change of our hearts.** If our hearts are not clean, if our hearts are not right, then everything else, from how we think, to what we say, to how we act and live, will be off-kilter. On one occasion, Jesus said, "It's not what goes in a man that defiles him or her, it's what comes out of the heart" (Matthew 15:11, author paraphrase). Jeremiah 17:9 says that, by nature, the heart is deceitful and desperately wicked. Our hearts have to be cleansed and changed and renewed by God's Word.

**4) David's prayer of repentance is a longing for the joy of God's presence.**

David basically says: "Do not cast me away from Your presence, And do not take Your Holy Spirit away from me. Restore to me the joy of Your salvation, And sustain me with a willing spirit" (Psalm 51:11-13, NASB 1995). If you love God and you sin, you'll want to run to Him in confession and repentance because you long for His presence and joy. Those of us who love God know how sin makes us feel. Our wrestle with the shame and guilt and even the struggle of our sin robs us of our joy and peace. We feel distant from God, and we don't want to be in that place; therefore, we run to God in confession and repentance to be close to Him and experience the joy and peace and gladness of His presence.

# CHAPTER 23

# PRACTICAL APPLICATION #7: WALKING WITH AND ABIDING IN GOD'S LOVE

We maintain close communion and fellowship with God when we **walk with God.** Enoch had a wonderful testimony as a man who walked with God (see Genesis 5:24), and he pleased God (see Hebrews 11:5). What does it mean to walk with God?

## WALKING WITH GOD BY OBEDIENCE

The prophet Amos asked the people of his day, "How can two walk together except they agreed?" (Amos 3:3, author paraphrase). No two people can have closeness and fellowship with each other if they are not in agreement. Walking with God means that we are in alignment with God's will and purpose for our life and allow the Holy Spirit to lead us. There's something about obedience to God's Word and walking in His will that enables us to experience His peace, joy, favor, and blessings unlike anything else, and even amid bad circumstances, we will not fear (or *should* not fear).

When I was very little in primary school, I remember a couple of kids who picked on me and threw food at me when we ate lunch. I was afraid of these two guys, but when the principal of the school noticed and came to the table, he made the two boys clean the food off of me and I was no longer afraid of them because I was with the principal. When we walk with God, we don't have to fear anything that may happen in our lives because God is with us, and we have the assurance that ALL things work together for good (even bad circumstances) to them who love God and are the called according to His purpose (see Romans 8:28). When we walk with God, we have His divine assurance of peace and faithfulness to work every situation out for our good, no matter what it is. **But note, God's promise in Romans 8:28 is not for everybody. It specifically says, "for them who love God and are the called according to His purpose."**

The proof of our love for God is found in our obedience to His Word. Jesus told His disciples: "If you love Me, you will keep My commandments" (John 14:15, NASB). Furthermore, we prove our love when we not only make Jesus our Savior but also our Lord through obedience to His Word. He told the people in Luke 6:46: "And why call me Lord and not do the things that I say?" (author paraphrase) Jesus emphasizes this in John 14:21 (NASB): "The one who has my commandments and keeps them is the one who loves Me; and the one who loves Me will be loved by My

Father, and I will love him and will reveal Myself to him." So, we commune and fellowship and walk with God by being obedient to His Word. When we are disobedient (especially willfully) and do not walk in God's will, we become disconnected from close communion and fellowship with God.

Jesus explains the benefit of obedience: "If you keep My commandments, you will abide [remain] in My love; just as I have kept My Father's commandments and abide [remain] in His love" (John 15:10, NASB 1995).

In other words, when we walk in obedience to God's Word and God's will, we receive the full provisional care, protection, and guidance of God's love.

## WALKING WITH GOD BY WISDOM

We maintain close communion and fellowship with God when we **live and walk by His wisdom.** Wisdom is taking knowledge and applying it in a practical way. Therefore, we walk by God's wisdom when we practically apply our knowledge of God from His Word to our lives and follow the Holy Spirit (see John 16:13; Galatians 5:16).

Shortly after young Solomon became the third king of Israel, God appeared to him in a dream and told him that whatever he asked for, He would give it to him. Of all things, Solomon asked God for a wise, discerning heart so he could rightly govern and judge the people of Israel as the new king (see 1 Kings 3:5-15). Because Solomon's request pleased God so much, he was granted what he asked for and became the wisest man who ever lived (see 1 Kings 3:12, 4:29-34), outside of Jesus Christ and God. God also gave Solomon things that he didn't ask for, such as wealth, honor, and the promise of a long life if he walked in obedience to God's guidance and instructions (see 1 Kings 3:13-14). You can probably imagine that Solomon was the subject matter expert on God's wisdom. Indeed, he had quite a lot to say about it Book of Proverbs, which largely consists of instructions on how to acquire and gain God's wisdom, the traits of a "wise" person versus a "foolish" person, the benefits of walking in God's wisdom, and the consequences of rejecting God's wisdom.

It's most vital and important to understand why it is essential to walk by God's wisdom and obedience to His Word and will for our lives: **because God our Creator loves us and knows, far better than we do, what is good and best for us.** In Proverbs 3:5-6, King Solomon says: "Trust in the LORD with all your heart, And lean not to your own understanding; In all your ways acknowledge Him and He shall direct your paths."

We acknowledge God by:

**1) Recognizing and surrendering to His Lordship in every area of our lives.**

Notice that Proverbs 3:5-6 did not say to acknowledge God in a few of your ways; it said, "in **ALL** your ways acknowledge God and He shall direct your paths." Sometimes we wonder why it seems that God hasn't given us His guidance and direction or why we haven't heard from Him. We might have to ask ourselves: "Have I or am I acknowledging God in ALL of my ways? Is there an area of my life that I haven't surrendered to the Lordship of God? Is there an area of my life where I have been disobedient to God's Word or am I walking outside of God's will?" God wants us to acknowledge Him in ALL of our ways. He desires to be

Lord over every area of our lives and when He is, He promises to direct our paths.

**2) Reverencing Him.**

We also acknowledge God by reverencing Him. We demonstrate reverence through honor and respect for God and through our praise and worship of God, but we also acknowledge God through our lifestyle when we live a lifestyle that brings glory and honor to Him.

**3) Obedience to Him.**

We acknowledge God by our obedience to Him. We may wonder why we haven't heard from God or why He hasn't given us guidance in a situation. In this case, we may have to ask: "Have I been disobedient to God in any way? Do I have any unrepentant sin in my life?" King Saul wondered why God had stopped speaking to him, and it was because he was disobedient to the previous instructions that God had given him (see 1 Samuel 15:11, 28:6).

I know I am walking in obedience to God's Word (God's will) and by His wisdom when I make wise godly decisions. I have such peace and joy from God, which are among the benefits of walking in God's wisdom (see Proverbs 3:2, 17). Proverbs 3:17 lets us know that God's wisdom paves a peaceful path for our lives. How can we know if we are making wise and godly decisions? Though not an exhaustive list, here are a few pointers:

- Is the decision you're about to make consistent with God's Word, nature, and character?
- Is the decision you're about to make a wise decision? (see Proverbs 2:11, 16). What are the benefits? What are the consequences of making this decision?

- Do you have God's peace about the decision you're making (see Colossians 3:15)?
- Have you sought out godly counseling on the decision? Counseling may not always be necessary, but sometimes it is good for us to first consult others we trust as a good source of godly counsel (see Psalms 1:1, Proverbs 15:22).
- Is the decision you're about to make the best or right timing? In Ecclesiastes, King Solomon says that a wise man will not only know the best course of action to take, but he'll also know the best timing for that course of action (see Ecclesiastes 8:5-6).

# CHAPTER 24

# PRACTICAL APPLICATION #8: HOLINESS (CONSECRATION)

Anything or anyone separate or set apart for the use and purposes of God is holy (see Leviticus 19:2, 20:7, 26, 21:8; Exodus 19:6). God is infinity holy from all His creation in that there is nothing or nobody else like Him (refer to attributes of God in Chapter 3). Another word for holiness is consecration. God is too holy to bear or tolerate sin in His presence (see Habakkuk 1:13). Therefore, we must also consecrate ourselves and live in holiness to have intimate, close fellowship with God (see Hebrews 12:14).

In his day, the Apostle Peter gives this charge of holy living to Christians:

> *Therefore, prepare your minds for action, keep sober in spirit, fix your hope completely on the grace to be brought to you at the revelation of Jesus Christ. As obedient children, do not be conformed to the former lusts which were yours in your ignorance, but like the Holy One who called you, be holy yourselves also in all your behavior; because it is written, "YOU SHALL BE HOLY, FOR I AM HOLY."*
> —1 Peter 1:13-16 (NASB)

Peter shares two practical ways for the Christians of his day (and for Christians today) to be holy. First, he mentions as obedient children of God, we should not be conformed to the former lusts (sinful desires) or as people driven by sinful desires before we came to God. As children of God, we need to genuinely live a life that is "set apart" from our old lifestyle and/or ways of sin to have a close, intimate fellowship and relationship with God. We should genuinely strive to live by God's ways and standards as found in His Word and not by our old sinful life or worldly standards.

Secondly, Peter tells Christians (then and now) that we should be holy as God is holy (see Leviticus 11:44). To "be holy" as God is holy is not just a one-time event; it consists of a daily and even life-long process of being transformed into the character and image of God (Jesus Christ). Yet this does not happen by our own strength and effort; it happens by the grace and power and transformation of the Holy Spirit's work in our lives, as we surrender in obedience to God's Word.

# CHAPTER 25

# PRACTICAL APPLICATION #9: BROKENNESS

We may not like to hear this, but our hurt, pain, and brokenness can draw us nearer to God. We arrive at a place of brokenness in our lives when we become so deflated or crushed (mentally, emotionally, or even spiritually) by something(s) that we recognize how much we really need God and turn to Him. In Psalm 51:17, King David acknowledges: "The sacrifices of God *are* a broken spirit, A broken and a contrite heart—These, O God, You will not despise." Psalm 34:18 (NIV) says: "The LORD is close to the brokenhearted and save those who are crushed in spirit." However, if we are not careful, we may turn away from God in our brokenness instead of to God to numb or bandage our brokenness, or self-medicate.

Our brokenness can be painful. Proverbs 18:14 (NASB) says: "The spirit of a person can endure his sickness, but *as for* a broken spirit, who can endure it?"

I remember when the screen on my old laptop broke. I saw all of these color bands and stripes across the screen. Because it was broken, it functioned in a way it was not originally made to function. When we experience brokenness, we often function in a way that is disparate to how God intended us to function. **We may indulge in certain patterns of behavior (e.g., drunkenness, see Proverbs 31:6-7) or other dysfunctional habits to fill a void in our lives with something that only God can fill.**

Brokenness can come in many forms. Our circumstances (e.g., loss of a job, loss of a loved one, loss of a relationship) can break us. An offense from another person or even our own sin and choices can break us. The Bible is full of people who loved and reverenced God but were broken and tried to cope with their brokenness in many ways.

- **Tremendous loss, grief, and depression broke Job.** Unforeseen circumstances of tragic loss and grief broke Job, inducing depression and suicidal thoughts (see Job 3:3, 4, 11, 25, 56).
- **Fear and depression broke Elijah:** Elijah is one of the greatest Old Testament prophets. He appeared in the transfiguration of Jesus along with Moses (see Matthew 17:1-3). He called fire down from heaven (see 2 Kings 1:12). He shut up and loosed the heavens with rain by the power of his prayers (see 1 Kings 17:1, 41-46; James 5:17-18). He had great victory on Mount Carmel in a contest against the prophets of Baal, proving that the one true God was the God

## PRACTICAL APPLICATION #9: BROKENNESS

who answers by fire (see 1 Kings 17:20-38). Yet, the words and actions of people broke even him, specifically those of King Ahab's wife, Jezebel, who threatened to kill Elijah. In fact, he was so broken that he ran away in fear for his life and fell into a deep depression (see 1 Kings 19:1-4).

- **The weight of ministry broke Jeremiah:** My mother named me (Jeremy) after Jeremiah, so he is one of my favorite people in the Bible. God foreknew Jeremiah before he was even born and had consecrated him in his mother's womb to be a prophet to the nations (see Jeremiah 1:5). Yet there came a time in Jeremiah's life when the weight of God's calling on his life as a prophet broke him. He felt like quitting because the people he preached God's Word to wouldn't listen or respond. Jeremiah was ridiculed and persecuted for preaching God's Word, yet even though he felt like quitting, he knew he could not quit because God's Word was like fire shut up in his bones (see Jeremiah 20:1-2, 7-10).
- **Sin and unwise choices broke David:** The weight and consequences of sin (shame, guilt, fear) broke David. His brokenness led him to turn to God for repentance and forgiveness of his sin (Refer to Practical Application #6 in Chapter 22).

**Broken things are often discarded or thrown away…but God!**

I sweep up the remains and discard a plate or glass that I've broken. Sadly, people are sometimes treated the same way. God still loves you when people write you off or discard you. You are not beyond the reach of God's love and grace. God will never write you off; God will never discard you or throw you away!

**Broken things are diminished in value... but God!**
Broken things are also often diminished in value, but it does not diminish your value or your purpose! Your value and purpose are in the God who created you, and even in your brokenness, God loves you, you matter to God, God still has a purpose for you and desires to restore you and make you whole when you are broken!

## EXAMPLE 1: THE PRODIGAL SON

Brokenness is sometimes necessary to bring us closer to God (or back to God, in some cases). Ecclesiastes 3:3 says there is a time to build up and a time to tear down; so, there is a time to be broken. For example, when we are prideful, puffed up, complacent in our own human strength, wisdom, ability, effort, and accomplishments, or intent on living and acting independently from God (as if we don't need Him), God may allow brokenness to humble us and help us realize that we do need Him so that we draw near to Him. This is exactly what happened to the prodigal son (see Luke 15:11-32). In this parable, the father represents God, and the young son represents us. The youngest son wanted to do his own thing, He felt he was big and bad enough to live and act independently from God and live life his own way. He took his father's full inheritance early and took off on a journey to a far country. There, he spent and squandered all that he had on reckless living. At that time, there was a severe famine in the land, and he was broke. Faced with his dire need, he found a job feeding pigs. He desired to eat the same pods that he fed the pigs (see Luke 15:16), and that is when he realized the gravity of his circumstances. His choices had broken him. His brokenness humbled the son, and he finally came to grips with his reality in verse 17: "He came to himself." **In other words, his breaking point was his turning point**. He ran back to his father who received him with open arms. That is just like God. No matter how far we have drifted, the arms of God's love and grace are always open for us to run to (or run back to), and that is why brokenness is sometimes necessary. Once we have drifted from God, we may not turn back until we experience brokenness. While we drift from God, our breaking point becomes our turning point.

## EXAMPLE 2: THE WOMAN WITH THE ISSUE OF BLOOD

Mark 5:25-34 tells the story of a hemorrhaging woman desperate for healing. She had been bleeding for twelve years and tried everything to bandage her brokenness; she went to every physician, she received every kind of treatment, and she spent all her money, but nothing worked. As a matter of fact, her condition worsened. I'm not saying you should never visit a doctor or physician to get treatment. We should pray and ask God to bring healing and make us whole, but not at the expense of neglecting practical solutions for health and healing. In other words, if you need to take medicine, take it! If you need to get treatment, get it! If you need that therapy session, get it! If you need grief counseling, get it! If you need a support group, go! If you need a doctor, go to the doctor! God can use or work through any of those things to help bring health and healing to you.

In 2017, I lost three beloved aunts (Aunt Evelyn, Aunt Sarah, and Aunt Juanita). Two of them died within a week of each other. My family had anticipated Aunt Evelyn's passing as she was in home hospice care. Yet as we were making funeral arrangements, my Aunt Sarah suddenly passed on a train traveling from New York within a week of Aunt Evelyn's passing. That week was very traumatic for me and my family. Later that year, Aunt Juanita passed away. These losses broke me. I depended on God's comfort and grace to get myself and my family through the grief, yet I had to do grief counseling. I found it very helpful to have a place where I could express and share my grief with others who were also grieving the loss of loved ones in full confidentiality. God worked through the grief counseling; through it, He brought me great comfort and mended my brokenness. The point is that God will use and work through practical methods of healing. At the same time, this passage illustrates that we can try all we know to do to cope with and bandage our brokenness, but ultimately it is Jesus who restores us and makes us whole. Even though I did something practical in taking grief counseling for the grief and loss of my aunts, I still give God the credit and glory for using grief counseling as a means to bring comfort and healing to my heart. I imagine the woman had heard testimonies about what Jesus did for them which gave her the hope and faith she needed to believe that if Jesus did it for that person, then He could do it for her. Indeed, when she reached out to Jesus in faith, she was made whole.

Many people (and perhaps you) appear fine or even great on the surface. They smile in their Facebook and Instagram pictures but are broken or hemorrhaging on the inside. God loves to use and restore broken things and broken people! **Jesus Himself was broken so we could be healed and made whole** as the Scripture in Isaiah 53:5 (author paraphrase) says: "But he was pierced for

## PRACTICAL APPLICATION #9: BROKENNESS

our sins, crushed for our iniquity. He bore the punishment that makes us whole, by his wounds we were healed." **God is still able and does heal us physically today, but what's better is that He will make us whole in all areas of life—physically, mentally, emotionally, and spiritually.**

# CHAPTER 26

# PRACTICAL APPLICATION #10: PUTTING ON THE FULL ARMOR OF GOD

Another critical way to keep your soul secure in God is by **PUTTING ON THE WHOLE ARMOR OF GOD.** The Bible says in Ephesians 6:11-12:

> *Put on the whole armor of God, that ye may be able to stand against the wiles of the devil. For we wrestle not against flesh and blood, but against principalities, against powers, against the rulers of the darkness of this world, against spiritual wickedness in high places.*

Satan (the devil) and his demons are referred to in this passage as "principalities," "powers," "rulers of the darkness of this world," and "spiritual wickedness in high places." In other words, they are **spiritual foes**. You cannot use physical means to defend yourself against them because they are spiritual threats. Instead, you must use God's spiritual armor and weapons to protect your soul from their evil schemes. **You must put on the whole armor of God**.

In ancient times, soldiers had to put on their WHOLE armor before a battle because the opposition looked for opportunities to attack them in their most vulnerable state. For example, if a man went to battle without a helmet or a breastplate, the opposition could strike a deathly blow to that soldier's unprotected head or chest.

As such, Paul instructed the church in Ephesus to put on the WHOLE armor of God so they would be able to stand firm against the wiles or schemes of the devil. Satan and his devils always look for opportunities to attack the Christian believer where and when they are most vulnerable. Therefore, whenever we fight or engage in spiritual warfare with Satan and his devils, we need to make sure we have on the WHOLE armor of God! Let us now take a look at each piece of the armor and their practical applications. Ephesians 6:14 (KJV) says: "Stand therefore, HAVING YOUR LOINS GIRT ABOUT WITH TRUTH…."

## THE BELT OF TRUTH

"Loins" refer to your midsection or waist area, the area between your hips and your ribs. In ancient biblical times, people "girded their loins" by tucking up the long, lower garments (clothing) with a belt around their waist so they wouldn't be too loose or floppy while traveling (see Exodus 12:11; 2 Kings 18:46, 9:1);

## PRACTICAL APPLICATION #10: PUTTING ON THE FULL ARMOR OF GOD

otherwise, their clothing could potentially hinder their mobility. The Roman soldiers wore a loosely draped, knee-length garment called a tunic. Since a significant part of ancient battles involved hand-to-hand combat, a loosely draped tunic was potentially dangerous because it could entangle them and hinder their mobility. Therefore, the first thing that a soldier would do before battle is "gird up his loins." Note that the first thing Paul mentions before any other piece of armor is to "HAVE OUR LOINS GIRDED ABOUT IN TRUTH."

Truth or truthfulness here is a virtue of Christian character. It conveys honesty and integrity; it is sincere, genuine devotion and commitment to live out the Christian life without hypocrisy or falsehood. To be successful in standing firm against the devil and his wiles in spiritual warfare, we must gird our loins in truth. That is, we must stand secure and firm in our devotion and commitment to God without hypocrisy based on His truth (the Bible). Our Christian life and walk with God must be authentic, sincere, and genuine; we must be cautious not to allow anything into our lives that would spiritually hinder or entangle our faithfulness and commitment to God with outside influences. Christians who are not secure or firm in their commitment to God or the truth of God's Word are akin to unprepared soldiers wearing loosely draped tunics that trip them up and open the door to spiritual attacks from the enemy (the devil). Therefore, in order to stand against the devil and his wiles in spiritual warfare, the first thing a Christian must do is remain secure and firm in their character of truthfulness as well as in the truth of God's Word.

## THE BREASTPLATE OF RIGHTEOUSNESS

The next piece of armor that Paul mentions is the BREASTPLATE OF RIGHTEOUSNESS. The breastplate was an important piece of the soldier's armor. It covered the torso, which contains vital organs such as the heart, lungs, liver, and kidneys. If a soldier were to fight in a battle without a breastplate, he would be vulnerable to having his vital organs pierced (by a sword, arrow, spear, javelin, or other deadly weapon) with a deathly blow from an opposing soldier. Going to battle without a breastplate would be like going on a suicide mission! Therefore when we engage in spiritual warfare with our enemy the devil—the enemy of both God and mankind—we need to ensure we have on our breastplate of righteousness, lest we give our enemy the devil an opportunity to strike a spiritual death blow to us!

How do we put on the breastplate of righteousness? Well, the devil comes to steal, kill, and destroy (John 10:10); he desires to bring death to us (i.e., spiritual death by separating us from God). Ultimately, Satan desires that mankind share in his eternal fate, which is forever separation from God and torment in the lake of fire. When our bodies die—the immaterial part of us—the soul and spirit separate from the body. So, spiritual death happens when we are separated from God. Adam and Eve had life in the Garden of Eden because they had a perfect relationship and fellowship with God. Nothing separated them from Him. Yet Satan, in the form of the serpent caused them to sin and disobey God because he desired to bring death upon Adam and Eve. And as a result of their sin, death came into the world. Adam and Eve eventually died physically, but they died spiritually the moment they sinned because their sins are what separated them from God.

## PRACTICAL APPLICATION #10: PUTTING ON THE FULL ARMOR OF GOD

In the end, they were expelled from the Garden of Eden, which is exactly what Satan desired.

The moment a person is saved through faith in Jesus Christ, eternal death no longer poses a threat to them because they have been given the promise of eternal life with God. So, if Satan can't bring eternal death to us, he will bring spiritual death to us in this life. He will attempt to break our closeness and fellowship with God through the temptation of sin, disobedience, and doubt because Satan knows that distance from God makes us vulnerable to his spiritual attacks.

Righteousness essentially means to be in right standing with God. We wouldn't need faith in the absence of sin—we would already be counted as righteous, justified, and innocent before God. Now, it is our faith that justifies us (makes us righteous) in the sight of God. Read the following passage:

> *What then shall we say that Abraham, our forefather according to the flesh, has found? For if Abraham was justified by works, he has something to boast about, but not before God. For what does the Scripture say?* "ABRAHAM BELIEVED GOD, AND IT WAS CREDITED TO HIM AS RIGHTEOUSNESS." *Now to the one who works, the wages are not credited as a favor, but as what is due. But to the one who does not work, but believes in Him who justifies the ungodly, his faith is credited as righteousness, just as David also speaks of the blessing of the person to whom God credits righteousness apart from works:* "BLESSED ARE THOSE WHOSE LAWLESS DEEDS HAVE BEEN FORGIVEN, AND WHOSE SINS HAVE BEEN COVERED. BLESSED IS THE

*MAN WHOSE SIN THE LORD WILL NOT TAKE INTO ACCOUNT.*—Romans 4:1-8 (NASB)

The Book of Romans has even more to say about righteousness: *If you confess with your mouth Jesus as Lord, and believe in your heart that God raised him from the dead, you will be saved; FOR WITH THE HEART A PERSON BELIEVES, RESULTING IN RIGHTEOUSNESS.* —Romans 10:9-10 (NASB, author emphasis added)

These passages teach us that the moment we believe that Jesus Christ died on the cross for our sins in our place and became our personal Lord and Savior, God will declare us righteous because of our faith (belief) in Jesus Christ. In other words, we are in right standing with God the moment we place our faith in Jesus Christ as our personal Lord and Savior. In that moment, we are justified and innocent in the sight of God. We could never earn righteousness by our own works, but because of our faith in Jesus Christ, God CREDITS us as righteous.

The word "CREDIT" in the first passage is a familiar term in the financial world; it means to take something (or someone) and credit it to another's account. For instance, a friend of mine knew that I loved browsing for books on Amazon, so she gave me an Amazon gift card with a $25 credit. I didn't do any work to earn this gift card; it was a free $25 gift credited to me to buy anything I wanted. In the same way, we can't earn righteousness by our own goodness, effort, or good works, but when we place our faith in Jesus Christ, God will CREDIT us as righteous on Jesus' account of what He did for us through His death, burial, and resurrection. This is what the scripture also teaches us about Abraham. Abraham was the father of the Jewish race and our example of faith because he believed in what God had promised him. So, God credited him as righteous because of his faith alone.

So, the first step to putting on the BREASTPLATE OF RIGHTEOUSNESS is placing your faith in Jesus Christ as your personal Lord and Savior to be instantly credited righteousness. In your righteousness, you can confidently stand before God without any shame or guilt because Christ paid your price by His death on the cross. His crucifixion has justified you and made you innocent before God. When Satan is on the attack, the Christian must be reminded and assured of who they are in God, through Jesus Christ who clothed them in His righteousness! As a believer, you will always have the promise of eternal life with God and will never be eternally separated from Him. Satan cannot threaten you with eternal death.

Nevertheless, even (and especially) as a Christian, Satan still tries to tempt and attack us to sabotage our relationship and fellowship with God. So, the second step of putting on (or keeping on) the breastplate of righteousness is to live a life of righteousness. We don't try to live a righteous life to be saved (Christ has already saved us), but we strive to live a righteous life *because* we are saved. Being righteous or living a righteous life means we strive to live and walk according to the Bible and the will of God for our lives (with the help and aid of the Holy Spirit).

Christians still sin because we have not yet been perfected into the ultimate likeness of Christ. As long as we live on this earth in our mortal frame, we remain a work in progress until we reach that perfection in Jesus Christ. We do not have a license to sin just because we know we are not perfect. As Christians, we all need to sincerely commit to a life of righteous, holy, and acceptable living that is pleasing to God. Nevertheless, because we are human, we will sin and fail. It's important to repent and confess our sins when we fail to maintain a close relationship and fellowship with God. Satan will use our refusal to confess and repent as a tool to distance us from God.

## FEET SHOD WITH THE PREPARATION OF THE GOSPEL OF PEACE

We've discussed the application of the belt of truth and the breastplate of righteousness for spiritual warfare. Next up is our feet—shod (or shoed) with the PREPARATION OF THE GOSPEL OF PEACE. In Paul's day, the Roman soldiers technically did not wear shoes or boots as we know them to be; rather, they wore sandals with leather straps. The straps were wrapped and fastened around their leg to hold the sole of the sandal firmly to the bottom of their feet. If you walk somewhere outside without shoes, you increase your chances of cutting or injuring your foot on something sharp. One time when I was little, I walked barefoot outside and accidentally stepped on a sharp nail. The pointed edge went straight up into the muscle of my foot; it wasn't a pleasant feeling at all. It hurt for several days, and it was a long time before I got up the nerve to walk outside without shoes!

Foot protection was also part of why soldiers wore the sandals they did. The opposing army might set traps or plant sharpened sticks in the ground to cause a serious foot injury or immobility to a barefoot soldier. A soldier also needed good traction if they

## PRACTICAL APPLICATION #10: PUTTING ON THE FULL ARMOR OF GOD

were on a slick surface or going up an inclined hill. Therefore, these sandals had flanged pieces of metal or nails at the bottom of the soles, similar to the cleats some athletes wear for traction. So, Paul's instruction speaks of the peace that we have with God through Jesus Christ. Romans 5:1-2 (KJV, author emphasis added) says, "Therefore being justified by faith, WE HAVE PEACE WITH GOD THROUGH OUR LORD JESUS CHRIST: By whom also we have access by faith into this grace wherein we stand, and rejoice in hope of the glory of God."

Peace with God means that God's wrath has been appeased or turned away from us because by faith in Jesus Christ, God's judgment and wrath are now reserved only for sinners. In contrast, we have PEACE with God. Now that we have peace with God we can also *experience* the peace of God. We can't experience the peace of God until we have made peace with God through Jesus Christ.

The peace of God gives us the ability to remain calm and assured in spite of life's circumstances and what the devil throws at us because we know that God is on our side, We know God is caring, loving, merciful, and gracious towards us, having all things and all power in His hands, and He promises to work all things together for the good to them that love Him and are called according to His purpose (Romans 8:28, author paraphrase). Our peace with God and the peace of God is what gives us the "traction" to stand firm in spiritual warfare against the wiles and attacks of the devil. Having our feet shod with the preparation of the gospel of peace gives us our confidence and assurance to stand firm against him.

## THE SHIELD OF FAITH

Paul instructs us to take up the SHIELD OF FAITH in order to QUENCH ALL THE FIERY DARTS OF THE EVIL ONE. The shield of a Roman soldier was a great piece of defensive equipment. It was large, wide, rectangular, and slightly curved so that the soldier could readily deflect opposing attacks. Additionally, the large shields were covered with leather which could be soaked in water to quench the fiery arrows (fiery darts) of an enemy. Sometimes the fiery darts that the devil launches at us come in the form of temptations. He may try to solicit or entice us to gratify our sinful desires rather than stay committed to God and depend on Him to meet our desires and needs (see Matthew 4). Sometimes his fiery darts come in the form of lies to cause us to doubt God, His goodness, and the promises found in His Word.

When the devil attacks us with his wiles, our faith in God and in the promises of His word is our shield and defense to quench all his fiery arrows. Hebrews 11:1 says: "Now faith is the substance of things hoped for, the evidence of things not seen" (KJV). The GNT translation (my paraphrase) says, "Faith is being sure for what we hope for, and being certain for what we cannot see." Consider the following. Let's say you know someone reliable and trustworthy (maybe a friend, parent, or sibling), and that person promised to get you an iPad for your birthday or Christmas. You don't possess the iPad the moment he or she promises it to you, but because the promise was made, you are confident that the iPad is yours.

If we can place our faith in a trustworthy person, surely we can place our faith in God and in what He has promised us in His

Word. Why? God is not a man that he should lie or fail or disappoint you or make mistakes as a man would (Numbers 23:19, author paraphrase). God is good, loving, merciful, caring, and gracious towards us. God is sovereign and desires the very best for you. He is always faithful to his Word; He can't break a promise because it is impossible for God to lie! Surely we can have faith in God and in what He has spoken and promised us in His word.

## THE HELMET OF SALVATION

The last piece of armor that Paul mentions is THE HELMET OF SALVATION. God's righteousness and salvation are like two sides of the same coin. While righteousness is justification (being in right standing with God), salvation is deliverance. Salvation means being saved, delivered, or rescued from something. Ultimately, the moment we place our faith in Jesus Christ as our personal Lord and Savior, not only does God CREDIT us as righteous, but He also gives us salvation to save, deliver, and rescue us from the guilt and punishment of our sins, which is eternal death (separation from God).

Helmets are highly encouraged in American culture for people who ride bikes or motorcycles because an injury to the head could be fatal. Of course, the helmets the Roman soldiers wore protected their heads from enemy attacks. Without a helmet, a soldier's head would be vulnerable to a fatal blow or beheading. The soldier would be at high risk of instant death.

Therefore, Paul instructs us Christian believers to put on the HELMET OF SALVATION, because our heads contain our minds—the center of our reasoning, our thinking, our thoughts, our will, and our emotions—which the devil often tries to attack and strike first. Our mind (heart) influences our thoughts, our speech, our conduct, our lifestyle, and our choices. In the Bible, Judas Iscariot betrayed Jesus because Satan had entered into his heart (see Luke 22:3). Judas allowed Satan to enter into his heart (his mind) to influence his thoughts and his will to betray Jesus. This is why our minds are the most important territory to defend. If the devil can get a hold of or control our minds, he can influence our reasoning, our thinking, our thoughts, our will, and our emotions—which is never a good thing! Therefore, the Bible warns us several times to guard our hearts and minds and keep them occupied with the right things and the right thoughts. Proverbs 4:23 (KJV, author emphasis) says, "KEEP THY HEART [mind] WITH ALL DILIGENCE; for out of it *are* the issues of life."

The charge to guard our minds is echoed elsewhere in scripture:

*And be not conformed to this world: BUT BE YE TRANSFORMED BY THE RENEWING OF YOUR MIND, that ye may prove what is that good, and acceptable, and perfect, will of God.—Romans 12:2 (KJV)*

Second Corinthians 10:3-5 (KJV, author emphasis added) says this:

*For though we walk in the flesh, we do not war after the flesh: (For the weapons of our warfare are not carnal, but mighty through God to the pulling down of strong holds;) CASTING DOWN IMAGINATIONS, AND EVERY HIGH THING THAT EXALTETH ITSELF AGAINST THE KNOWLEDGE OF GOD, AND BRINGING IN CAPTIVITY EVERY THOUGHT TO THE OBEDIENCE OF CHRIST.*

## PRACTICAL APPLICATION #10: PUTTING ON THE FULL ARMOR OF GOD

Paul continues in the Book of Philippians:

*Finally, brethren, whatsoever things are true, whatsoever things are honest, whatsoever things are just, whatsoever things are pure, whatsoever things are lovely, whatsoever things are of good report; if there be any virtue, and if there be any praise, THINK ON THESE THINGS.—Philippians 4:8 (KJV, author emphasis added)*

When we apply clothing ourselves with the helmet of salvation, we protect them from the lies of the devil. We guard against all negativity and ungodly things that can take root in our minds. At times, we may find ourselves wrestling with the lies of the devil, with fear, doubt, negativity, and ungodly thoughts, so we must put on our helmets to bind and submit them to God. The helmet keeps our minds renewed and refreshed with the assurance of the promises and blessings of God's Word.

The Bible says: "For as he [a man] thinks in his heart, so *is* he!" (Proverbs 23:7.) In other words, if we think like a defeated person, before long we will begin to talk and act like a defeated person and be conformed into a defeated person. If we think like a sad and depressed person, before long we will begin to talk and act like a sad and depressed person and be conformed into a sad and depressed person. This is why Paul encourages us to be TRANSFORMED BY THE RENEWING OF OUR MINDS and not CONFORMED in our minds. Conformity (change from the outside in) is when we allow the lies of the devil, the world, the appearance of circumstances, and life to dictate how we think. Conversely, transformation (change from the inside out) is when we allow the Word of God to dictate how we think, which will in turn dictate our circumstances and our lives.

## MENTAL STRONGHOLDS

Second Corinthians 10:4-5 tells us:

*For the weapons of our warfare are not carnal but mighty in God for pulling down strongholds, casting down arguments and every high thing that exalts itself against the knowledge of God, bringing every thought into captivity to the obedience of Christ.*

We must be mindful and aware of mental strongholds that can capture our thoughts and shape them into ungodly thought patterns that dictate our actions and even our lifestyles. In the Bible, strongholds are walls or defensive structures of refuge. They fortified a city. Second Samuel 5:9 says that King David lived in a stronghold because he had built walls around the city he lived in. Those walls protected him (and the people in the city). When the Apostle Paul wrote to the Corinthian church, they were familiar with the concept of a stronghold because they had an acropolis in their city (Corinth) which was a high, fortified place with thick stone walls they could escape to if they ever needed to retreat.

You will find in scripture that "stronghold" is used metaphorically like in the verse above. The verse also insinuates that a stronghold can be either positive or negative. In addition to protection, a stronghold also denotes a prison or place of bondage. These are the strongholds the Apostle Paul encourages us to knock down. Other translations use the word "demolish," as in a complete demolition. If you have ever seen the demolition of a wall or a building where the whole structure comes crashing down, this is what a demolition of mental strongholds should look like.

Notice what the Apostle Paul says in verse 4, that the weapons of our warfare are not carnal, but they are mighty in God for

## PRACTICAL APPLICATION #10: PUTTING ON THE FULL ARMOR OF GOD

pulling down (or demolishing) strongholds in our lives. In ancient warfare, when an army attacked a fortified city, they couldn't just go up to the city and push the gates or doors open because they were locked from inside of the city. They needed something massive like a battering ram to break through or demolish the doors or walls. The Apostle Paul uses a similar illustration to say that we cannot demolish formidable strongholds fortified in our minds with our own human strength, efforts, and reasoning; we need weapons that are mighty in God to demolish them.

The Apostle Paul asserts that these strongholds imprison people and teaches the Corinthian church how to deal with them in verse 5. He says to "cast down arguments and every high thing that exalts itself against the knowledge of God, bringing every thought into captivity to the obedience of Christ." Therefore, strongholds may be a cycle, pattern, behavior, or lifestyle that we feel hopeless in or in bondage to because we have allowed our thoughts to be enslaved to an argument or a way of thinking. These arguments that have been so deeply entrenched and fortified in our minds could be based on human philosophy or reasoning, lies or deception, fear, doubt, or unbelief, but when we allow these arguments to barricade our thoughts from the truth and knowledge of God's Word, then they have become strongholds in our minds.

Therefore, the Apostle Paul says we have to cast down or demolish these fortified arguments so that our thoughts can be reprogrammed based on the knowledge and truth of God's Word, and that is what it means to bring every thought into captivity, unto the obedience of Christ. We have to surrender our thoughts to Christ. We have to allow the Lordship of Christ and His Word to take control of our thoughts instead of every high thing that exalts itself against the knowledge of God because we live out what we think and how we think. Proverbs 23:7 says: "As a he [a man] thinks in his heart, so *is* he." When you think like a defeated person, you're going to talk and act and live like a defeated person. We often struggle more than we have to or more than we should because of what we think and how we think, so these strongholds begin and end in the mind.

Numbers 13:30-14:4 shows us the type of mindset that the children of Israel had even after they had seen and experienced God's miraculous deliverance out of Egyptian bondage and slavery. They had seen God's mighty hand at work time and time again, yet they still had a mindset based on their fear, doubt, and unbelief that often led them to grumble and complain. Notice some of the arguments they made based on their way of thinking in Numbers 4:2-3 (author paraphrase):

"If only we had died in Egypt or in the Wilderness!"

"Why has the Lord brought us to this land to die?"

"Wouldn't it be better for us to return to Egypt?"

These were the typical arguments that had been so entrenched and fortified in their minds that they ran from the giants, doubting whether the land God had promised them was their land after all. The problem was their mindset; it kept them from advancing into the place God wanted to take them.

From this example, we see that a lot of the strongholds we face are strongholds that we have erected in our own minds. I had a loved one who was in a very bad relationship. The guy was no good for her and did not treat her well, yet I would hear her say things like: "I love him.... he loves me.... I can't leave him."

## PRACTICAL APPLICATION #10: PUTTING ON THE FULL ARMOR OF GOD

Her reasoning puzzled me deeply. It didn't make sense, but it was a stronghold so deeply entrenched and fortified in her precious mind that she thought this guy loved her. She didn't feel like she could leave him and didn't believe she could do better or deserved better, so she remained in that cycle of allowing men to mistreat her.

The Apostle Paul tells us how to practically demolish strongholds that have been fortified in our minds. He says to cast down imaginations (arguments) because as Christians, God has given us the authority and power to do what He says we can do. We may not always use it. We may not always recognize it, and sometimes we may even question or doubt it, but if you are a child of God, you have the authority and power to do what God says you can do (not in your own strength, but by depending and relying on God's grace and power), including controlling your thought life. Temperance (self-control) is a fruit of the Spirit, and so if we have God's Holy Spirit and God's Word, we have what we need to take control of our thought life instead of allowing our thoughts to take control of us.

Every day, we have to choose whether we will give our thoughts over to anxiety, stress, depression, fear, doubt, unbelief, or ungodly philosophy or surrender our thoughts to the Lordship of Christ and His Word. I've struggled with strongholds in my life at times. I would cry my eyes out to God and exclaim, "Lord! It seems I cannot shake this cycle or pattern!" but God would respond, "I've already made a way of escape for you; all you have to do is just surrender to Me, surrender that area of your life to Me, surrender that situation to Me." As I meditated on God's Word and prayed, I realized the pattern came from my thinking, but

God had given me the authority and power to cast it down by His Holy Spirit and by the power of His Living Word. I realized I didn't have to keep thinking that way, so as I surrendered my thoughts to the Lordship of Christ, transformation took place in that area of my life.

I share all these things not to bring anyone under condemnation who may be wrestling or struggling with his or her thinking because we all struggle with it. We've all felt hopeless, helpless, guilty, and ashamed about our struggles or the strongholds in our lives. We all ask ourselves, "Will I ever overcome this? Will I ever break this cycle or pattern?" Yes, I am talking about people who love God. First Corinthians 10:13 (NIV) says: "No temptation has overtaken you except what is common to mankind. And God is faithful; he will not let you be tempted beyond what you can bear. But when you are tempted, he will also provide a way out so that you can endure it."

Our addictions, struggles, or strongholds are not unique. Someone else has struggled with the same things or may be struggling with them as we speak. God has delivered and set someone free from them, and He can and is willing to do the same for you because God is always faithful to make a way of escape; we may not always take it, and sometimes we even like to wallow in our misery, but there is always a way of escape, and that way of escape is surrendering to God's way.

Finally, Romans 12:2 says: "And do not be conformed to this world, but be transformed by the renewing of your mind, that you may prove what is that good and acceptable and perfect will of God." I like to think of it this way: **conformation is a change that takes place from the outside in, but transformation is a**

PRACTICAL APPLICATION #10: PUTTING ON THE FULL ARMOR OF GOD

**change that takes place from the inside out. A life change or transformation must first take place in our minds.** We can assert our intentions to change our behaviors all day long, and we may even succeed for a little while, but if the transformation hasn't first taken place in our minds, then those changes will be temporary. So, how do we renew our minds? **With God's Word! We must filter, surrender, and align our thoughts to what God says in His Word. That is how we put on and keep on our helmet of salvation!**

# PRACTICAL APPLICATIONS SUMMARY

We've discussed what it means to abide in the secret place of the Most High. It's not a physical location but a lifestyle of closeness and intimate communion, fellowship, and relationship with God. To achieve these things, we need to apply ten essential practices to our daily lives:

- Practical Application #1: A Strong Prayer Life
- Practical Application #2: Fasting
- Practical Application #3: Genuine and True Worship
- Practical Application #4: Genuine Praise
- Practical Application #5: Abiding in Christ
- Practical Application #6: Confession and Repentance of Sin
- Practical Application #7: Walking with and Abiding in God's Love
- Practical Application #8: Holiness (Consecration)
- Practical Application #9: Brokenness
- Practical Application #10: Putting on the Full Armor of God

# LIVING IN THE SAFETY OF **GOD'S SECRET PLACE**

I highly encourage you to read through all of Psalm 91. Meditate on the benefits of abiding in the secret place of the Most High and making God your refuge (i.e. deliverance, God's help and victory over circumstances and the devil's schemes, God's presence in trouble, God's faithfulness to answer prayer.. to mention a few) . Let's end with two.

Verse 3 says: "He will protect you from the snare of the fowler" (author paraphrase). A fowler is someone who sets traps to catch birds. It could even describe a hunter who sets traps to catch animals for food. The fowlers in your life may be people who have ill will towards you or try and make your life miserable, but when you abide in the secret place of the Most High, God has a way of keeping and preserving you from their schemes and plots against you, including the devil's!

Verse 11 says, "He will give His angels charge concerning you, To guard you in all your ways" (NASB 1995). God has used the ministry of angels in my life to keep and protect me from harm, both seen and unseen. When the devil tried to kill me and my mom in a car wreck about fourteen years ago, we were able to walk away from the accident. The car was totaled, but we had no scars or injuries because of the ministry of angels that intervened that day! God will give His angels charge concerning you! Those are only a few of the many benefits we have in God when we abide in the secret place and make God our refuge. Amen!